F

THE BIRDER'S MISCELLANY

A Fascinating Collection of Facts, Figures, and Folklore from the World of Birds

SCOTT WEIDENSAUL

A FIRESIDE BOOK
Published by Simon & Schuster Inc.
New York   London   Toronto   Sydney   Tokyo   Singapore

A RUNNING HEADS BOOK

Copyright © 1991 by Running Heads Incorporated

Fireside
Simon & Schuster Building
Rockefeller Center
1230 Avenue of the Americas
New York, NY 10020

THE BIRDER'S MISCELLANY
was produced by Running Heads Incorporated
55 West 21 Street
New York, NY 10010

Editor: Charles A. de Kay
Designer: Helene Berinsky
Managing Editor: Lindsey Crittenden

10 9 8 7 6 5 4 3 2 1

Library of Congress Cataloging in Publication Data

Weidensaul, Scott.
    The birder's miscellany : a fascinating collection of facts,
figures, and folklore from the world of birds / Scott Weidensaul.
        p.   cm.
    "A Fireside book."
    Includes bibliographical references and index.
    ISBN 0-671-69505-3 : $9.95
    1. Birds—Miscellanea.   2. Birds—Folklore—Miscellanea.
I. Title.
QL676.W395   1990
598—dc20   90-45414
                                                    CIP

Typeset by David E. Seham Associates

To my parents,
for tolerating—let's face it—a pretty weird kid.

◆   ◆   ◆

With sincere thanks to Charlie deKay at Running Heads and Edward Walters at Fireside, whose direction and enlightened editing made this book much better than it would otherwise have been; and especially to Sheila Buff for guidance, support, and a really big leg up.

CONTENTS

INTRODUCTION

A number of years ago, a friend with only a marginal interest in the outdoors started telling me excitedly about a nature show she'd watched on television the evening before. The program traced the lives of desert animals, and included a segment on the Namaqua sandgrouse of the Kalahari Desert in Africa. Every day for weeks, the male sandgrouse flies as much as a hundred miles to waterholes, soaks his breast feathers and carries the precious water back to his nestlings, who must have it to survive.

"That's absolutely incredible!" my friend said breathlessly, her eyes suddenly opened to the wonder of birds.

She was right, and in a broader sense than she realized. Birds are incredible animals—incredible in the ways they have adapted to their environments, from polar ice packs and deserts to steamy rain forests; incredible in their beauty; their migration paths; their ways of courting, nesting, feeding, and moving. One bird, the peregrine falcon, can dive at speeds of more than 200 mph. Hummingbirds can fly backwards. Male emperor penguins incubate their single egg on their feet for two months, mostly without moving, through the bitter Antarctic winter. Incredible.

The snippets of information that follow represent only a fraction of the intriguing things we know about birds, as science and amateur observation unlock their secrets. We now know that even the most commonplace birds do marvelous things, like the young warblers that each autumn fly, in a single, unguided hop, from New England backyards across the open sea to Venezuela. In the end, the most remarkable thing we've learned may be that there are no *un*remarkable birds—that each, in its own way, lives an astounding life.

1

— ♪ 1 ♪ —

SIZES, SHAPES, AND COLORS

At less than 2 grams—lighter than a dime—the Cuban bee hummingbird is the smallest bird in the world, and one of the smallest vertebrates in existence. Its length is just about $2\frac{1}{2}$ inches (compared to 4 or 5 inches for most North American hummers) and that total includes the long, thin bill used for sipping nectar.

Because it is warm-blooded, there is a limit to how small a hummingbird can be, since the smaller a creature is, the more heat-dissipating skin it has in relation to heat-producing body mass. Apparently, the bee hummingbird is as far down the scale as nature can go in the bird department; any smaller, and the hummer's metabolism would not be able to keep up with the demands for heat. But there appear to be few other limits, for the number of forms, colors, and shapes that birds take at times seems infinite.

♦   ♦   ♦

The Biggest Bird

The prize for largest bird is contentious, depending on how one defines "large." In terms of wingspan, the marabou stork of Africa and the wandering albatross of the Southern Hemisphere, with wings stretching almost 12 feet, are tops; the Andean and California condors, at 9 feet, are runners-up. In terms of weight, however, the flightless os-trich (which can, after all, afford a few extra pounds), leads the pack at 350 pounds. Even that impressive figure is eclipsed by the extinct elephant bird of Madagascar, which, judging from its massive skeletal remains, weighed 950 pounds. The honors for the tallest bird go to another extinct species, the moa of New Zealand, which—at 13 feet tall—must have towered over the aboriginal humans that hunted it into extinction. The tallest living species is the ostrich, roughly half the size of the moa.

The heaviest flying bird appears to be the mute swan; one enormous male tipped the scale at just over 50 pounds, more than double the weight of the average condor. Mute swans are, however, rather sedentary birds, while condors spend much of their time on the wing.

Eggs Great and Small

Not surprisingly, the elephant bird also laid the largest known bird egg, more than 14 inches long and probably weighing about 27 pounds; with the elephant bird's extinction, the record devolves to the ostrich egg, 6 inches long and $3\frac{1}{2}$ pounds in weight. The smallest egg is the vervain hummingbird's, less than half an inch in length—and $\frac{1}{5,500}$th the mass of the ostrich egg.

For an elephant bird that weighs a half-ton, a 27-pound egg makes sense biologically; it's a mere $\frac{1}{35}$th of the bird's mass. The goldcrest of Europe, a close relative of North America's golden-crowned kinglet, is a $3\frac{1}{2}$-inch-long songbird that lays a clutch of ten eggs that, in total, weigh 144 percent of their mother's body weight. Even more remarkable, the female goldcrest lays the clutch in just ten days.

Teeth

"Scarce as hen's teeth" is rare indeed. No bird has true teeth, but some have bill adaptations that fill a toothy role.

The mergansers, fish-eating ducks

EGG SIZES

Generally, the bigger the bird, the smaller each egg is in comparison to the mother's body weight. This chart shows the changing proportions, from the ostrich to the almost painfully big egg of the kiwi.

Bird	Percentage of female's body weight
Ostrich	1.7
Bald eagle	2.4
Albatross	6.0
House wren	13.0
Northern fulmar	15.0
Storm-petrel	22.0
Kiwi	25.0

found throughout the Northern Hemisphere, have toothlike serrations along the edges of their bills that allow them to grasp slippery prey firmly while diving in fast-flowing water. Toucans, with their enormous, colorful beaks, use the jagged edges of the upper mandible to slice off pieces of the fruit on which they feed.

Both the tongue and upper mandible of a flamingo have rows of toothlike strainers that permit the bird to feed in its unique way. In a sense, the flamingo eats upside down; when it stretches its neck down to the water, the down-curved portion of the bill is perpendicular to the surface. The flamingo then opens and shuts its mouth rapidly, pumping muddy water through the strainers and filtering out algae, crustaceans, and other tiny organisms.

Birds of Paradise

No other family of birds is so gloriously arrayed as the birds of paradise, native to Papua New Guinea and surrounding islands. Their colors and forms of their plumes are so bizarrely beautiful that, when the first skins of some species arrived in Europe in the 1800s, naturalists insisted that they were fakes, concocted from the feathers of many birds.

But real they are. The best known is probably the greater bird of paradise, about 18 inches long. Nearly half that length is taken up by the bird's long, gauzy flank feathers, which cascade back and down like a red-gold waterfall. Others are much smaller, like the King of Saxony bird of paradise, a sparrow-sized bird with a rather conservative black and yellow pattern—conservative, that is, except for the two 18-inch-long crest feathers that arch back from its head like feather pens tucked behind a scribe's ears. The streamer quills bear 30 or more small "flags" that are bright blue on one side and brown on the other.

The extraordinary is ordinary among birds of paradise, many of which look as if they were designed by a crazed artist with no sense of color composition. The male of the superb bird of paradise, black with a greenish cap, can raise a fan of black feathers behind the head that is almost as wide as he is long. A somewhat smaller fan of greenish blue breast feathers can also be raised, all but encasing the bird's head in a sort of feathered clamshell. The Wilson's bird of paradise has a bare head like a medieval monk wearing a tonsure; the bright blue skin has a crosslike design of black on it. The rest of the bird is equally outlandish—a yellow back, red rump, green breast and two curling, blue tail plumes that twist forward like springs.

The bright colors of this family belong to the males; females are dull and brown. The colors and feathers are obviously a secondary sex characteristic for attracting a mate (the long plumes are molted after the breeding season), although no one is sure why the birds of paradise have carried them to such extremes. Few species have been thoroughly studied in the thick, wet jungles of New Guinea, but many of those that have display communally on a shared courtship ground. Among the greater bird of paradise, the males assemble in a tree that has been stripped of leaves. Here they raise their trembling flank feathers over their heads while fanning their wings forward, all the while jumping from perch to perch to the accompaniment of their loud calls. Such breeding assemblies, called leks, are also common among grouse, hummingbirds, and shorebirds, but they are especially valuable in jungles, where visibility is limited. Rather than wasting energy and time hunting all over for a mate, a female can come to a traditional lek and simply pick the most vigorous male available. The union lasts only seconds, then the female goes on her way, probably never to see her mate again.

Who's Who?

Because individual birds of the same species are usually identical to the human eye, scientists have long sought ways to tell one from the other, hoping to decipher the mysteries of longevity, migration, and mating habits. To that end they have banded birds' legs, clipped colored streamers to their wings, even painted them with harmless dyes. The birds can be forgiven for taking offense.

But the late Sir Peter Scott, founder of the Wildfowl Trust in Slimbridge, England, discovered that such intrusive methods are not necessary with one British bird. The Bewick's swan (now considered conspecific with the tundra swan of North America), has a patch of yellow at the base of its black bill. Watching the hundreds of swans at Slimbridge, Scott realized that each had a unique facial pattern, and that by starting a photo file of swan heads, he could track the comings and goings of individuals in this species, which nests in arctic Siberia.

The Basis for Color

Color is not always what it seems, especially on birds, among the world's most splendidly arrayed creatures.

On most birds, colors come from pigments in the feathers, substances that *absorb* part of the "white" sunlight hitting them, then *reflect* a select portion of the color spectrum, which to the observer's eye is the "color" one sees. Pigments known as melanins produce the blacks, browns, grays, and beige tones, while carotenoid pigments are responsible for the yellows, reds, and oranges.

The head plumes and multicolored bill of this tufted puffin are seasonal ornaments only; the plumes and white facial feathers molt out at the end of the breeding season, while the largest of the bill scales fall off.

Research has shown that birds cannot produce their own carotenoid pigments; they rely on their food for these chemicals. A change in diet, therefore, may mean a change of color. Canaries deprived of the class of carotenoids called xanthophylls in seed will become white, and captive flamingos that aren't fed enough carotenoid-rich crustaceans turn a washed-out shade of pink.

There are other pigments as well, many of them only now being recognized. But blue, which is a common color in birds, stems not from a pigment at all, but from the structure of special cells in the feather barbs. Microscopic box cells *scatter* the light that hits them, favoring shorter blue wavelengths, while an underlying layer of melanin absorbs any of the longer red wavelengths. Called Tyndall scattering, it works on the same principle that causes the sky to be blue because of atmospheric interference. When combined with yellow carotenoid pigment, scattering also produces most of the greens that birds show.

The last source of color on birds is *iridescence,* another mechanical, rather than chemical, phenomenon. The best examples are the hummingbirds, which among the more than 300 species bear virtually every combination of iridescent coloration. As with scattering, iridescence is a result of feather structure. Specialized feather cells split the sunlight into the spectrum, reinforcing some wavelengths and nullifying others through spectral interference. The resulting colors have a neon intensity, but unlike pigmented color, or even scattered blue, iridescent colors are totally dependent on the angle

of the light. A hummingbird properly aligned with the sun will shimmer brightly, but if it turns just a little bit the wrong way, the fire will go black.

Out of Sight, Out of Mind

The brightly colored hummingbirds and parrots are well known for their beauty, but many birds make a habit of staying out of sight. The whip-poor-will of North America is one, so perfectly camouflaged against the dead leaves of its oak forest habitat—its plumage a cryptic mixture of brown, white, buff, and black—that it is almost invisible, even at extremely close range. In the same Eastern forests, the ruffed grouse nests on the ground, where it is at the mercy of every passing fox, owl, or raccoon. The grouse is exceptionally well camouflaged, however, affording it a measure of protection during its three-week incubation period.

The killdeer, a shorebird common over most of North America, would not at first seem to be camouflaged at all, since it has a pure white breast crossed by two brown bands. But like a zebra's stripes, the bands break up the killdeer's outline against the pastures and fields where the bird lives, providing what is known as disruptive coloration—and excellent protection.

The plumage of the black-billed magpie shows all three forms of coloration: pigmentation in the black head and back, Tyndall scattering on the blue secondary wing feathers, and iridescence where the long tail feathers shimmer green and bronze. The engraving is based on an Audubon painting.

Shorebirds, like these spotted sandpipers (in an engraving based on an Audubon painting), show how "evolutionarily plastic" bills and feet are adapted to help the bird fit a particular ecological niche, which in the case of the spotted sandpiper is foraging along stream and pond banks for insects.

Even the brilliant colors of tropical species function as a form of camouflage. In the world of flickering highlights and deep green shadows of the rain forest, the splashes of reds, yellows, and greens blend with the background surprisingly well, so that it is really quite difficult to see even the most garish species.

Tail? What Tail?

A male peafowl, iridescent green feathers raised in a magnificent halo around his head, is an arresting sight. But the train he proudly displays is not his tail;

it is actually a set of greatly elongated upper tail coverts, or "rump" feathers. His true tail is a set of drab, stiff feathers that help brace the raised train.

Bills and Feet

A bird's beak and legs are, as biologists say, "evolutionarily plastic" features, changing easily with the shifting demands of the environment. The result is a bewildering assortment of beaks and feet for every purpose, from chiseling to paddling to snowshoeing to probing to killing.

Watch a mixed flock of shorebirds

John James Audubon depicted an adult golden eagle clutching a snowshoe hare, graphically rendering the powerful, taloned feet on this magnificent bird of prey. Raptors—hawks, eagles, falcons, vultures, and owls—have disparate evolutionary backgrounds, but are united by their feet and beaks, which are uniquely adapted for hunting.

along a tidal mud flat, and you'll see that each species has a bill-and-leg combination for a unique feeding niche. The avocet, which feeds on invertebrates in several inches of water, has long legs and an extremely long, thin bill that curves up at the end so the tip is perpendicular to the water when the bird leans over to feed. The ruddy turnstone, on the other hand, feeds above the tidal line, so it needs only short legs. Its bill is also short and stout, perfectly suited for flipping over small rocks and shells to uncover insects and crustaceans beneath. Dowitchers have long, straight bills for probing through flooded mud flats for food, while the long-billed curlew, with a down-curved beak almost as long as its body, digs even deeper for its prey. Such resource partitioning keeps each species from competing directly with the others for the limited food supply.

Eyesight and Hearing

Hawks, eagles, and falcons live by their eyes, scanning vast distances for prey. Their eyesight is superb, although the usual comparison, that it equals a human's with 8-power binoculars, is misleading. It's not that a hawk enjoys magnified vision, but that its ability to discriminate detail over distance is vastly better than a person's. Thus, a red-tailed hawk kiting 1,500 feet above the ground can spot a rabbit scurrying through the underbrush, where a human would see only an indistinct jumble of shapes and colors at that range.

Within the hawk's eye itself, the thickest concentration of sensory cells is in the upper half of the retina, which detects objects on the ground. When a hawk is perched and wants to watch something flying overhead, it frequently twists its neck so that its head is upside down, bringing the object under the scrutiny of the more sensitive upper half of the eye.

Even birds that don't hunt for a living have sharper vision than most people. One way to tell is to microscopi-

A raptor, like this immature goshawk, has more than one million vision cells per square millimeter in each eye. This affords the bird roughly eight times the visual acuity of humans.

cally examine the fovea, the region of the eye with the best visual acuity. A hawk has about 1,000,000 visual cells per square millimeter in the fovea, while humans have about 200,000.

Hunting in murky twilight or full dark, owls obviously need excellent night sight, which explains their oversized eyes. But there is a tradeoff—good night vision requires an abundance of the visual cells known as rods, which detect low light levels, as opposed to cones, which function best at higher light levels. Cones are also best at discriminating shapes and colors, so an owl can see well in the dim light of moon and stars, but cannot discern details nearly as well as most birds. Even worse, the large size of the eye means a reduction in the owl's field of view, so that it goes through life with a form of tunnel vision.

If their vision is worse than some birds', the owl's hearing is unparalleled.

9

The Pelican's Bill

Yes, as a matter of fact, a pelican's "bill can hold more than its belly can"—about three gallons of liquid in the pouch of a white pelican, compared to a stomach capacity of a little more than a gallon. That's no problem for the pelican, since the pouch (more properly called a gular sac) is designed to act as a scoop when the bird is fishing, and the water is immediately drained away before the fish are swallowed.

There are two North American species of pelicans, the familiar brown pelican of the southern and western coasts, and the white pelican that breeds across much of the West and Great Plains. The white, the larger of the two, develops a shaggy crest and bright orange beak in the breeding season; the beak also sprouts a horny vertical plate whose function is unclear. The brown pelican molts a set of brown and yellow neck feathers for courtship and its beak turns grayer, but it grows no plate.

The two species both eat fish that they scoop up in their expandable pouches, but they hunt in different ways. The brown pelican is a plunge feeder, diving from several yards above the water. As the bird hits it throws its wings back for better streamlining, and opens its cavernous maw into a school of fish. From below the water, it looks like the Attack of the Carnivorous Umbrella. The white pelican is too buoyant to dive, so it sedately dips for fish from the surface. A flock will often cooperate by corralling a school in shallow water. Because habitat requirements for feeding differ from that of nesting, the white pelican may fly as much as 150 miles each day between its nest and its feeding grounds.

Most of the time, the pleated skin of a brown pelican's throat gives little hint of the tremendous size to which it can expand.

The round, flat facial disc that surrounds the eyes serves as a sound collector, funneling the waves into the ear openings, located under the feathers beside the eyes. In some owls, like the boreal owl of Canada and Alaska, the ear openings are asymmetrical—the right ear hole points up, while the left one points down. This helps the owl pinpoint sound even more precisely.

The erect feather tufts on the heads of great horned, screech, and long-eared owls are frequently mistaken for the birds' actual ears. They are not. The tufts, which can be raised or lowered at will, serve as camouflage (by breaking up the owl's outline) and possibly as a way of communicating.

Touchy-feely Feeding

For birds that hunt for prey they cannot see, having a sense of touch in the bill is a big advantage. The woodcock, an upland sandpiper common in the Northeast, feeds on earthworms, which it plucks up from deep underground with its long bill. The woodcock apparently senses the worm with nerves in the end of its beak. The bill is further specialized by having a flexible tip, which can open underground just enough to pinch the worm.

The black skimmer, a large tern of the Atlantic and Gulf coasts, also has nerve endings in its unusual, knife-shaped beak. The skimmer's lower mandible is several inches longer than the upper beak. When fishing, the skimmer flaps slowly along the surface of the water, with just the tip of the lower bill cutting a wake. When the bird touches a small fish, the beak automatically trips shut, pinning the prey. The lower bill also grows faster than the upper bill, compensating for the constant friction from water, which would otherwise wear the beak away to a stub.

The roseate spoonbill of the American tropics, like its Old World relatives, has a spatulate bill that it swings from side to side through muddy water, rapidly opening and closing it, much as a flamingo does. Any small fish, crustacean, or insect that the spoonbill feels is instantly gulped down, along with a fair bit of suspended debris. The stomachs of dissected spoonbills usually contain mostly mud, with only a small percentage of food.

The Colorful Bill of the Puffin

In most species the bill is strictly utilitarian, but for puffins—those roly-poly seabirds of the Northern Hemisphere—the bill is an important courtship feature.

Through the long winter, which the puffin passes on the high seas, the bill is rather small and very dull, with little of the brilliant colors it bears in summer. But as the days lengthen toward spring, scales on the beak begin to form and thicken, growing into plates of red, yellow, and blue (two other, smaller scales form around the eye of the Atlantic and horned puffins, while the tufted puffin of the Pacific grows long yellow head tufts instead).

As soon as the breeding season ends in August, the scales are shed. Scientists consider this a primitive throwback to the puffin's reptilian ancestors, which also shed scales periodically.

A Swainson's hawk in Montana shows the armament essential to a hunter—a hooked beak for tearing meat into bite-sized pieces, and taloned feet that do the actual killing—as it screams at an intruder that has wandered too close to its kill.

Golden Slippers and Other Bird Feet

Feet play an equally diverse role in a bird's life. In winter, the ruffed grouse grows tiny, horny fringes on its toes that function as snowshoes to spread the bird's weight out over the snow and prevent it from sinking. The feet of grebes and loons are lobed for powerful swimming strokes, and of course the webbed feet of ducks, geese, and swans perform a similar function. Snowy egrets have yellow feet—"golden slippers," to bird watchers—that startle minnows out of hiding. A woodpecker's feet are large and zygodactylous—that is, arranged with two toes pointing for-ward and two to the back, each with a large claw for clinging to a vertical tree trunk. The feet of flightless birds like the ostrich and emu are heavy and almost mammalian for stability, although the cassowary of Australia and New Guinea has retained a long, sharp inner claw that the bird uses to kick its enemies with deadly effects; over the years, many people have been killed by these aggressive birds.

Birds of prey have some of the most highly adapted feet in the bird world. A golden eagle has feet with long, curving talons, backed by powerful tendons that drive the knives deep into prey. The osprey, which hunts only fish, has a further refinement: tiny spikes on the soles of the feet that act as a nonslip surface for gripping fish.

A few birds, so at ease in the air that they rarely sit, have all but dispensed with feet. Chimney swifts have clawed feet for perching inside hollow trees and masonry chimneys, but they cannot walk. Neither can most hummingbirds, which must take off and land to move even an inch or two.

The jaçanas, a family of small marsh birds, have adapted the snowshoe idea for their own use in the tropics. The trick to survival here is not to avoid sinking in snow, but to stay above the water's surface, and the robin-sized jaçanas have solved it by developing excessively long toes, up to $2\frac{1}{2}$ inches in length. By spreading their weight over a very wide area, the jaçanas can scamper over lily pads and other floating vegetation, where birds with shorter toes would immediately sink.

◆　◆　◆

While hummingbirds have heart rates as high as 1,200 beats per minute, large, ground-dwelling birds like the wild turkey (here, in Audubon's famous portrait) have much slower rates—about 90 beats per minute, in the case of the turkey.

The Heart of the Matter

Generally speaking, the smaller the bird, the bigger its heart—in proportion to its body size, that is. The heart of the tinamou, a large, sluggish forest fowl of South America, is just .21 percent of its body weight. A hummingbird, however, which has a ferocious metabolism and a circulatory system to match, has a heart that makes up 2.4 percent of its mass—proportionately

HEART AND RESPIRATION RATES

With one exception, these figures represent birds at rest, expressed in beats or respirations per minute.

HEART RATE

Domestic turkey	93
American crow	342
European starling	460
Black-capped chickadee	500
American robin	570
Blue-throated hummingbird (in nighttime dormancy)	36
Blue-throated hummingbird (at rest)	480
Blue-throated hummingbird (in flight)	1,200

RESPIRATION

Red-shouldered hawk	34
American robin	45
Northern cardinal	45
House wren	83
European starling	84
Northern oriole	107

more than ten times greater than the tinamou's. The hummer's heart rate is also far faster; a blue-throated hummingbird, in active flight around its Southwestern habitat, has a pulse rate of nearly 1,200 beats per minute. A turkey's heart barely exceeds 90.

A hummingbird burns a tremendous number of calories each hour, and must feed frequently just to break even metabolically. Nighttime in the warm tropics is no hazard, but for hummingbirds that live high up in mountains like the Andes and the Rockies, eight frigid hours without food can be fatal. So some of these hummers drop into a hibernationlike torpor, lowering their respiration, heartbeat, and metabolic rate for the night and conserving their energy reserves. However, females incubating eggs do not do this, since they must maintain their body temperature for the sake of the eggs. Apparently, the thick walls of their spider web-and-lichen nests provide enough insulation to protect them from the cold.

Sleeping the Winter Away

Native American people of Arizona long believed that some birds slept through the winter in rock crevices, much the same as marmots and chipmunks hibernate below ground. As the science of ornithology grew during the nineteenth century, the old belief that birds could hibernate was ridiculed.

Then came the winter of 1946, and the discovery of a common poorwill (a close relative of the whip-poor-will) jammed in a rock cleft in Arizona, deep in dormancy. Its body temperature was just 64 degrees, far below normal; it had no detectable heartbeat or respiration. The Native Americans were right.

It is now known that wild poorwills can go for more than three months in such a deathlike state. Called hypothermism (as opposed to mammalian hibernation), it is largely a response not to cold, but to lack of food. In experiments, poorwills will not enter dormancy until they have lost 20 percent of their body weight. Brought into a warm room, the bird recovers it senses quickly. In addition to poorwills and some hummingbirds, a few swifts are also known to enter a torpor when starving, although for much shorter periods of time.

Feather Types

Feathers are not created equal. There are, in fact, six major varieties, with an almost infinite number of variations, each for a specific purpose.

Contour feathers cover a bird's body, providing streamlining and, in the case of the stiff flight feathers, the lift needed to get off the ground. To keep the feather smooth and uniform, each thin barbule has a row of tiny hooks that zip it fast to the next barbule. Beneath the contour feathers are *down* feathers, very light and fluffy because the individual barbules of the feather do not lock together. Their purpose is to insulate the bird with trapped air, which is why down is used for human insulation, too.

Semiplume feathers are a combination of a contour feather with a downy base, and are often found on the sides and back of a bird. *Filoplumes* are thin and hairlike, and because they are scattered among the flight feathers, and have a sophisticated network of nerves at their base, are believed to help the bird adjust the larger flight feathers. *Bristles,* specialized feathers that look like stiff hairs, surround the mouths of such insect eaters as swifts and nighthawks, acting as a funnel. In the nostrils of ostriches, they are dust filters.

The oddest feather type is *powder down,* which constantly sheds its minute tips, giving the bird's plumage a chalky surface. Not all birds have powder down feathers, and those that do, such as herons and bitterns, appear to gain waterproofing from them.

◆　◆　◆

2

FLIGHT, MOVEMENT, AND MIGRATION

The premier ability of a bird is its command of the air—flight. Not every species can fly, nor do all have the same speed or skill aloft, but no other group of living things is so much a part of the sky.

Because they fly, birds are found in virtually every corner of the globe, crossing oceans, deserts, and ice packs with equal ease. One species of skua has even been seen over the South Pole, a bleak place otherwise devoid of vertebrate life. The migrations of birds are epic; only the travels of pelagic fish and a few of the great whales can compare.

♦ ♦ ♦

The First Feathers

Feathers, the hallmark of the Class Aves, are an evolutionary variation on the reptilian scale. But what a variation! Both are made of keratin—a hard, horny substance—and on some parts of a bird's body (the legs, for instance) there is little difference between a lizard's scales and the bird's. Feathers, on the other hand, are a world apart. Every bird possesses them, and no other living thing has them. There has been a lot of debate over the years as to the reason why some small, agile, and possibly warm-blooded dinosaurs developed feathers and the ability to fly. Some scientists contend that feathers were originally for insulating arboreal dinosaurs, and only later came into use for flight as the protobirds glided from tree to tree. Others, drawing their conclusions from the fossil *Archaeopteryx*, argued that flight feathers evolved as a sort of flyswatter, used by ground-dwelling, insect-eating dinosaurs. That theory was eventually discredited, but it is now widely be-

With its long, tapered wings and deeply forked tail, the American swallow-tailed kite of the Southeast is one of the most graceful of fliers, capable of snatching dragonflies from the air, as well as reptiles and amphibians, as depicted by Audubon.

lieved—based on a study of the movement of flying birds—that the forerunners of birds were indeed swift, ground-dwelling dinosaurs, rather than species that lived in trees and glided.

Getting Off the Ground

Besides evolving feathers, birds have developed a couple of other essential adaptations for flight. A deep sternum, or breastbone, anchors the flight muscles. The other bones are hollow, for weight reduction (a feature virtually lacking in a few birds, like gulls and penguins),

but are reinforced with struts for greater strength. A system of air sacs throughout the body further reduces weight. The upshot is a creature that weighs less than its size would indicate. A live golden eagle with a 7-foot wingspan will weigh an average of just 10 pounds, while the skeleton of a frigatebird with a comparable wingspan weighs just 4 ounces.

Fast, Faster, Fastest

The record for fastest bird is murky. The top spot has long been given to

17

the brown-throated spinetail swift, for which a speed of 218 mph was claimed in 1922. But the two swifts whose flight was being timed (in the Cachar Hills of India) actually disappeared from view for some time behind a ridge, thus leaving the veracity of the claim in serious doubt.

There can be no doubt that the peregrine falcon is fast, and many authorities consider it the world's fastest living creature. In level flight the peregrine is not particularly speedy; migration studies at Pennsylvania's famed Hawk Mountain Sanctuary showed that migrating peregrines moved along the ridge at between 20 and 40 mph, while other studies suggest a range of 40 to 60 mph for cruising flight.

That changes when a peregrine gets hungry. Like all falcons, the peregrine is streamlined, designed for blistering aerial attacks on its prey. It may try to outfly its quarry in level flight, but more often the falcon will climb high, then drop in a "stoop," or attacking dive. The peregrine gives a few final wingbeats as the dive begins, then folds its wings. It may drop for a thousand feet or more, gathering momentum and exceeding 200 mph as it closes with the hapless shorebird, duck, or songbird.

Everything about a peregrine is built for speed. The close-fitting and smooth contour feathers of the body minimize wing drag. Special baffles in the nostrils allow the bird to breathe at extreme speeds, and muscles in the eye permit rapid focus changes as the falcon roars down on its prey. The kill may come from a raking slash with the talons or a blow from the partly clenched feet, knocking the smaller

bird senseless while the falcon swoops out of the dive to retrieve its meal.

Speed Demons and Slowpokes

Measuring the speeds of flying birds is a highly imprecise science because of such factors as head or tail winds, barometric pressure, and the age of the bird. And there is no way to know if the bird is flying at top speed or merely cruising along at a more leisurely clip. Nevertheless, over the years many species have been timed in flight from cars and planes, and the speeds, while only rough estimates, give an idea of what different families can do. The red-

---

FLIGHT SPEEDS

Speeds are given in miles per hour, and are usually the result of rather imprecise field estimates.

Ruby-throated hummingbird	27
American robin	32
Horned lark	54
Killdeer	55
European starling	55
Barn swallow	60
Mallard	60
Oldsquaw	72
Canvasback	72
Lammergeier vulture	80
Red-breasted merganser	80
Common loon	90
Domestic racing pigeon	94
Peregrine falcon (in dive)	217

Hummingbirds are the only birds that can hover and fly backwards, thanks to an unusual arrangement of fused wing bones, flexible joints, and powerful chest muscles. To hover, the bird holds its body vertically and flaps in a figure eight, like a swimmer treading water.

throated loon of the arctic, for example, has been timed flying at 56 mph, almost the same speed as the smaller, more aerodynamic wood duck and killdeer, both at 55 mph. A robin has been measured at about 30 (and can probably fly faster), while the tiny chipping sparrow can also probably exceed the 20 mph it is credited with. Among waterfowl, the red-breasted merganser can hit 80 mph, while the canvasback can reach a slightly less impressive 72.

The faults of timing a bird from inside a car are demonstrated by ruby-throated hummingbirds. For years their top speed was considered to be more than 50 mph, the same as a Can-

ada goose, based on observations from a moving automobile. But experiments in wind tunnels showed that a ruby-throat could not make headway against a wind of more than 27 mph, suggesting that the bird in the earlier measurement was getting an assist from a tail wind.

Up, Down, and Sideways

The hummingbirds are the only vertebrates in the world that can hover in one place or fly backwards, and they do it with a very special arrangement of bones, muscles, and feathers. Think of the bones in a bird's wing as analogous to those in a human arm and hand. A hummingbird's "arm" bones—the humerus, radius and ulna—are very short and are fused together, so that there is almost no movement of the elbow and wrist. However the carpals, or "finger" bones to which the flight feathers are attached, are very long. In addition, the shoulder girdle is very flexible, allowing the hummer to freely move the wing both horizontally and vertically.

To hover, the hummingbird holds its body vertically and flaps its wings in a shallow, horizontal figure eight, forcing air up on the backstroke and down on the forward stroke. The effect is very much like a person treading water in a pool, using their hands to maintain position. Reverse flight requires a back-reaching stroke of the wings, like a swimmer doing a backstroke. To keep the wings in motion—usually 50 to 60 beats a second, and sometimes as many as 200—the hummingbird has proportionately massive chest muscles compared to other birds.

Highs and Lows

The highest-flying birds ever recorded were a flock of geese over Dehra Dun, India, at an altitude of 29,700 feet. Alpine choughs, small crowlike birds of Asia, have been seen at the top of Mount Everest, at more than 29,000 feet, and the massive lammergeier vulture has been seen at 25,000 feet in the Himalayas. In the Western Hemisphere the record may be held by the Andean condor, which has been spotted at 19,800 feet.

Small birds are also capable of flying to high altitudes. Many of the warblers and vireos that breed in the eastern United States and Canada strike out in autumn across the U.S. continental shelf and the Caribbean, flying over water until they hit the South American coast. Radar studies in the Antilles show that the migrant flocks maintain an average altitude of about 9,000 feet, although some have been known to fly as high as 21,000 feet. Such high-altitude flight is physically demanding for a bird of any size, but especially a songbird. They are somewhat protected from the extreme cold by their feathers, but breathing frigid air puts a strain on their system. Much worse are the effects of diminished air pressure and oxygen content. To stay aloft a bird must flap harder and faster than at lower altitudes, but at the same time there is less oxygen in each breath to fuel the engine. On the positive side, migrating birds may find favorable tail winds at high altitudes, or less turbulence than is present near the ground.

At the opposite extreme, depth recorders fitted to emperor penguins show this Antarctic species dives as deep as 875 feet, where they feed on squid. It is possible they can dive even deeper when not encumbered by scientific apparatus.

Nonstop Terns

The long distance champion among birds is the arctic tern, which breeds across the top of the Northern Hemisphere. Those terns from the eastern North American arctic, Greenland, and northern Europe funnel east and south

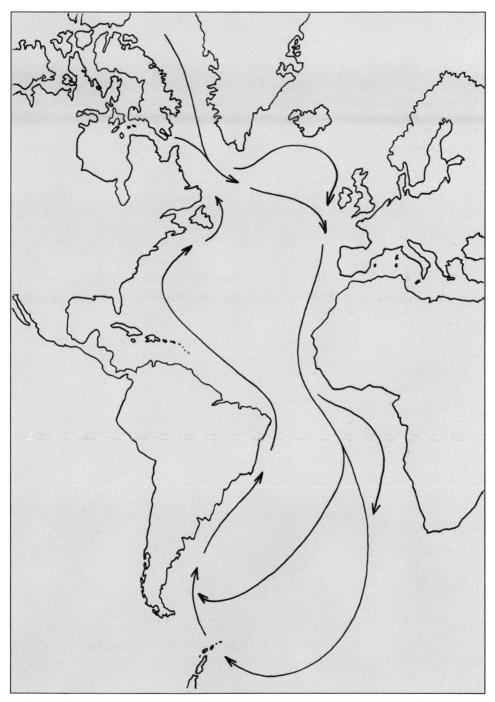

The arctic tern is the world's long-distance champ among birds, flying a 22,000-mile loop each year.

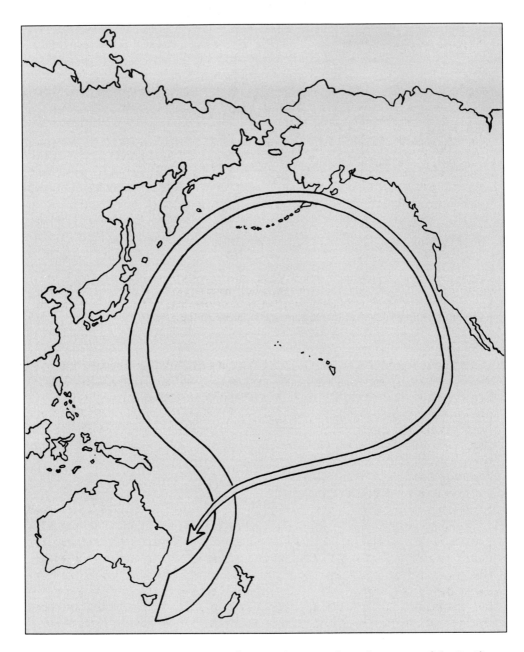

The short-tailed shearwater inscribes a figure eight across the wide expanse of the Pacific during its annual migration.

Canada geese—among the most vocal of North America's wild birds—use their loud, two-note *ha-RONK!* to maintain contact with other flock members and to warn of danger. Geese have a number of other vocalizations, including a low feeding murmur and a menacing hiss given by either sex if an intruder comes too close to the nest.

in late summer, passing by Britain and Spain, then along the west coast of Africa and down to the edge of Antarctica in time for the austral summer. Then, in the austral fall they apparently loop north along the coasts of South and North America in time for another breeding season in the arctic, completing a circular route of more than twenty-two thousand miles.

As impressive as the arctic tern's migration may be, other birds spend even more time on the wing. Many species of albatrosses, petrels, and tropical terns spend their first several years at sea, not coming to land until they have reached maturity. Some can rest on the water, but the sooty tern quickly becomes waterlogged, suggesting that it spends virtually its entire first six to eight years in ceaseless flight.

Other long-haul migrants include the bristle-thighed curlew, which breeds in Alaska and winters in Polyne-sia, an over-water trek of more than six thousand miles. Some of the lesser golden plovers that nest in Alaska also strike out across the Pacific, stopping two thousand miles later in Hawaii.

Loop the Loop

The short-tailed shearwater breeds off the southern coast of Australia, then follows a figure eight migration each year. Starting in March, after the breeding season, the shearwater loops east to New Zealand, then curves back northwest in Japan by May. Late summer finds the birds in the Bering Sea moving east, down the coasts of Alaska and British Columbia in September, then striking out southeast over open water in October to return to the breeding grounds for the start of nesting in November. Total distance: twenty thousand miles.

Have Goose, Will Travel

Hummingbirds are the smallest birds in North America, but that doesn't stop several of them from migrating vast distances. The rufous hummingbird travels north each spring from central Mexico to as far as southeastern Alaska. The rufous travels by land, however, and can stop frequently to rest and feed. The ruby-throated hummingbird of the East crosses the Gulf of Mexico on its fall migration, a distance of more than five hundred miles. For years this was considered impossible, based on estimates of a hummingbird's fat reserves and the number of calories such a water crossing would require. When it became obvious that the hummers were accomplishing the feat anyway, the biologists rechecked their figures and discovered that they had miscalculated.

Some hummingbirds may hitchhike south. A number of reports, most of them anecdotal, tell of migrating geese being shot which, on closer examination, were found to have torpid hummingbirds nestled beneath their back feathers; one such incident is said to have occurred in British Columbia in 1936. If real, these tales are reminiscent of the old Chippewa Indian legend of the golden eagle that thought it had won a contest to see which bird could fly highest, only to have a sparrow leap off its back at the top and fly on to the edge of the sky.

Up the Down Mountain

Journeys need not be long-distance to qualify as migrations. Many alpine birds drop to lower elevations in winter to escape the cold and snow, a phenomenon known as vertical migration. But the blue grouse of the western United States and Canadian ranges has a unique twist on this routine—a reverse vertical migration. In spring the grouse inhabit mid-level deciduous forests, feeding on buds, flowers, and new leaves. As summer comes the females drop even farther into the valleys, their chicks in tow, to feed on berries and insects. When autumn returns, however, the grouse begin to drift higher into the mountains again, and by the time the snows fall they have climbed into the highest alpine conifer forests, where spruce and fir needles comprise a large part of their diet.

Irruptive Migrations

The goshawk of the northern forests is only partially migratory; some birds drop south for the winter, while others stay on their breeding grounds year-round. But every ten or eleven years there is a major southward invasion of goshawks, possibly caused by a cyclic crash in the populations of snowshoe hares and grouse, their main foods. During such irruptions (as they are correctly known) goshawks may be found as far south as Florida.

Many other boreal and arctic species are irruptive. The snowy owl is usually nonmigratory, but the low point in the lemming cycle will send thousands of these big, white owls into southern Canada and the northern United States. Great gray, boreal, and hawk owls irrupt periodically, although in smaller numbers.

The snowy owl of the arctic is not migratory, but every few years thousands of them "irrupt" south, forced by the threat of starvation when the lemming, the owl's main food, hits the low point in its life cycle. Pioneering bird artist Alexander Wilson painted this snowy owl in the early 1800s, along with a male kestrel.

Migration Paths

Although they can cross large bodies of water, most migrating birds prefer to avoid doing so. For that reason, migration routes often bend to take advantage of islands, peninsulas, and shorelines. Birds flying south along the Atlantic coast funnel into the peninsula of Cape May, New Jersey, before heading out over the thirteen miles of Delaware Bay. Likewise, Point Pelee, Ontario, another long, narrow peninsula, is the first landfall for songbirds crossing Lake Erie going north.

Tropical Havens

The rain forests of the tropics are vital not only to the birds that live there year-round, but to hundreds of species that migrate from North America each autumn. Thrushes, tanagers, vireos, warblers, orioles, swallows, hummingbirds, and many other varieties rely on undisturbed forests for their survival.

Many North American breeding birds undergo a change of diet or behavior when they reach their tropical wintering grounds. The eastern kingbird, an insect eater in the north, switches over to almost nothing but fruit, and times its migration with the ripening of favorite species like the *Cecropia* tree. Obviously, the loss of the tropical forest will have a grave effect on birds like the kingbird, and it seems likely that the alarming declines in neotropical migrants are directly linked to the rampant deforestation of Central and South America.

The Once and Future Migration

How does a migration start? Scientists have long speculated that migratory routes build slowly, as generation after generation of birds probe into new territory, then retreat to an ancestral winter home over an ever-lengthening path. This would account for the large number of birds with tropical roots that now breed in the northern United States and Canada, presumably having followed the retreating glaciers after the last ice age.

This process of expanding into new areas is still occurring, and can be seen in several arctic species. One is the pectoral sandpiper, which nests in the North American arctic from Ontario to Alaska, and winters in southern South America. Pectoral sandpipers are also found along the shores of the Arctic Ocean in the Soviet Union, but in the fall, instead of going south into Asia or Africa, the Siberian race travels east across the Bering Strait and joins the North American population on its trek.

The wheatear is another arctic species, a black-and-white thrush. There are two North American populations; one breeds in Alaska, the other in the eastern arctic of Canada. Both populations winter in Africa (the only North American species to do so), but they get there by different routes. The Alaskan birds go west to Siberia, then south through Asia to Tanzania, while the eastern birds hop to Greenland, Iceland, Europe, and finally to the western edge of Africa.

Not every bird follows the same route both north and south, although most do. The lesser golden plover comes north from Brazil and Argentina across South America, up the Central

Topographical features—mountains, lakes, rivers, peninsulas—often concentrate bird migrations in a phenomenon biologists refer to as "leading lines." At Hawk Mountain Sanctuary in Pennsylvania, migrating birds of prey follow the sinuous Kittatinny Ridge, which deflects the wind and provides a reliable source of updrafts.

American isthmus and on to the arctic across the heartland of the United States and Canada. It does not return that way, however, but detours far to the east, through Quebec, Labrador, and Newfoundland, where it finds an abundance of berries on which to fatten before flying south across the Atlantic to the shores of Venezuela.

Why not take the shorter over-water route to Labrador in the spring, too? The Canadian Maritimes are notoriously foggy and cold then, and there would be little in the way of food for the exhausted migrants. The central, land-based route, on the other hand, offers warmth and food in the spring.

Cold weather is not the only thing that prompts a migration. The beautiful pennant-winged nightjar of Africa, a relative of the nighthawk with long, trailing wing feathers, follows the rainy season around the continent. It breeds in southern Africa during that region's rains, roughly from September through November, then wanders north to the Equator to central Africa in February, when that area gets its rains. The reason? The wet weather brings out mating swarms of flying termites, the nightjar's main food.

Navigation on the Fly

One of the abiding mysteries of migration is how a bird navigates. Decades of research have finally unearthed some of the answers.

Birds apparently navigate using one or more of five main information sources—the sun, stars, topographic features, the earth's magnetic field, and odors. Solar and stellar positions seem to be the most widely used (and most accurate) navigation tool, especially for songbirds. In experiments conducted in planetariums, caged songbirds correctly oriented themselves with the pole, even if they had never seen the sky. If the sky is overcast, migrant birds may switch to wind direction or topography, but this often leads them astray, especially at night, when most songbirds migrate.

Pigeons, petrels, and a few other seabirds have been shown to navigate by odor, at least near the nest, and homing pigeons have been experimentally shown to be able to use the planet's magnetic field to find their way home. How much these two senses are used by other birds, however, is still open to debate. A recent study of bobolinks revealed that they have a deposit of magnetite, a magnetized iron oxide, next to nerve tissue in the head, which may be used for navigation. In experiments, captive bobolinks detected changes in artificial magnetic fields, and this built-in compass probably allows them to do the same thing in the wild.

It is clear that a migratory bird is born with the instinct to migrate, and an innate knowledge of where to go. Migratory birds held in captivity will grow restless during spring and fall, reacting to changes in the amount of sunshine rather than temperature or food. Likewise, few birds migrate in family groups, or even flocks of mixed-age birds, in which older individuals could show the young where to go for the winter. Indeed, in many species it is the youngsters who leave the breeding grounds first, to be followed weeks later by the adults.

♦　♦　♦

Waterfowl, like these Canada geese by Audubon, usually follow distinct flyways on their annual migrations. Because of their importance to sport, waterfowl have been more intensely studied—their intricate wanderings more carefully plotted—than any other group of wild birds.

Highways in the Sky

Because waterfowl are of tremendous sporting and economic importance, their migration has been studied better than any other group of North American birds. From banding returns, radio-telemetry and observation, it is clear that the continent is crossed by several major "flyways"—aerial paths followed by the birds for generations.

The Atlantic flyway draws ducks and

29

geese from New England, the eastern arctic, and the tundra along the west edge of Hudson's Bay; the primary species are wood ducks, mallards, black ducks, snow geese, and some divers. The birds funnel south through the mid-Atlantic region to the coast. The Mississippi Flyway is perhaps the biggest, with millions of waterfowl following the river's course to the Gulf of Mexico. The Central Flyway, running through the Plains states and Rocky Mountain foothills to Texas, attracts Canada and white-fronted geese, gadwall, redheads, mallards, shovelers, and others. The Pacific Flyway, famous for its pintail flights, covers the area from the Rocky Mountains west to the sea, and hosts most of Alaska's migrant waterfowl.

There is plenty of overlap between the flyways, especially in the more northern areas. Some species that breed in a rather restricted region may even follow different routes south. One is the Ross' goose, a smaller version of the snow goose. Those Ross' that breed on Queen Maude Gulf in the Northwest Territories follow the Pacific Flyway to California, while those that breed just several hundred miles away on Hudson's Bay take the Mississippi Flyway to Louisiana.

Home Is Where the Heart Is

Homing instinct can bring a bird home over great distances, even if it has been displaced by man. A Manx shearwater, heartlessly taken from its nest burrow in Skokholm Island off Wales and airfreighted to Boston, was released. It

crossed the 3,100 miles of open ocean in twelve and a half days—a blistering average pace of 248 miles per day. A Laysan albatross shipped 3,200 miles from its breeding place was back in ten days, and a European alpine swift needed just three days to cross the thousand miles it had been moved.

Winter at Sea

The open sea in winter is a frigid, inhospitable place in the north, but that doesn't stop birds from passing the season there. Puffins, murres, and other auks disperse from their cliffside breeding colonies in late summer and spend the next eight months far out of sight of land. So do such sea ducks as the oldsquaw, scoters, and some eiders; others, like the harlequin duck, stay within sight of land during the winter, feeding on mollusks that live beneath storm-lashed jetties.

Among the daintiest of these oceanic birds are the storm-petrels and phalaropes. Leach's storm-petrel is a tube-nose, scarcely bigger than a swallow, that breeds in the Canadian Maritimes and along the Pacific Coast. In winter it drops south to both coasts of South America. The red phalarope, a shorebird also of swallowlike dimensions, winters at sea from California south to South America, feeding on plankton at the ocean's surface.

Diving for Food

Nearly 400 species of birds swim, and about 150 catch their food by diving for

The double-crested cormorant is a diver, using its webbed feet to propel it underwater on its hunt for fish. To help it sink, a cormorant's feathers are not waterproof, so it must spread its wings to dry when it has finished fishing. Small flocks of cormorants, sitting spread-eagle in the sun, are a common sight along freshwater rivers and lakes.

it. Plunge divers, like brown pelicans, gannets, and terns, drop head first into the water and are carried several feet down by the momentum of their fall. Others, like loons, use their lobed or webbed feet to dive to much greater depths for fish; loons can stay submerged for up to fifteen minutes, and have been caught in fishing nets set 180 feet deep. Still other species, like the auks of the Northern Hemisphere, swim by flapping their wings underwater. Because water is so much denser than air, their wings must be thinner and shorter than those of birds that do not fly submerged, yet the wings must also be big enough to support the bird

aloft. The wings of the Atlantic puffin, a common auk, are therefore a compromise between sea and sky.

Penguins are the birds most superbly adapted to the water. Streamlined and flightless, they are clumsy on land but can porpoise effortlessly through the water in pursuit of krill and small fish.

Penguins are descended from flighted birds (the embryonic chick grows, then loses, flight feathers), but this group of fifteen species made the evolutionary choice of water over air more than 50 million years ago. They have changed little since then, although their habitat has altered dramatically, in one of the raw deals nature routinely hands its creatures. What was once a warm, subtropical environment has now become much colder, especially for the emperor and Adelie penguins of the Antarctic.

Because penguins don't have to worry about becoming airborne, they can be much heavier than flighted birds (the emperor penguin weighs about 75 pounds). Their wings have evolved into flippers very similar to the long, tapered appendages of some whales, and their feathers, instead of growing in distinct tracts, are spread evenly over the bird's entire body. The feathers are oily and dense, providing an impervious layer of trapped air, an excellent insulator, between the bird's body and the freezing water.

Most people think of penguins as strictly Antarctic, but the family is widespread through the Southern Hemisphere. Jackass penguins live in South Africa, Magellan penguins on the coast of South America, and tiny blue penguins in Australia and New Zealand.

Rails, as a family, have an extremely high rate of flightlessness, especially among island species isolated from predators. Even flighted species, like these clapper rails, common to the salt marshes of both coasts of America, prefer to walk through dense marsh vegetation than to fly.

Flightless Birds

At first thought, a bird that can't fly would seem to be at a great disadvantage, unable to migrate or escape its enemies easily. Yet there are a great many flightless birds in the world, from the massive ostriches and emus to tiny flightless rails. There are flightless ducks, cormorants, grebes, a flightless parrot, and a wren. The three species of kiwi in New Zealand are among the oddest of the lot, with their hairlike plumage and long, curved beaks. Rails—weak fliers in the best of circumstances—are a family with a high degree of flightlessness, with sixteen living and twelve extinct species. One of the most beautiful is the takahe, a rare blue and green bird with a heavy red bill found on New Zealand's South Island.

Under the right conditions, the inability to fly is no detriment to a bird. The biggest precondition seems to be a lack of land predators, which is why so many flightless birds evolved on islands where there were no predacious mammals. All modern flightless birds evolved from flighted ancestors, and it seems that the ability to get off the ground is shed quickly in a predator-free environment, since many relatively young islands have flightless species closely related to flying mainland forms. Naturally, the introduction of predators can be disastrous, and many flightless species have become extinct because of rats, pigs, dogs, house cats, snakes, and other alien predators let loose by visiting humans. Such was the fate of the Stephen Island (New Zealand) wren, killed off by a lighthouse keeper's cat in the 1890s.

Man has also killed off many flightless birds directly. The moas and elephant bird, the largest birds ever, were early casualties of aboriginal hunters. The dodo and its relatives, the solitaires, of Mauritius, were gone by 1700, killed by European sailors hungry for meat. A similar fate befell the giant auk, a flightless seabird of the north Atlantic. In all, 16 of the 62 known modern flightless birds are now extinct, unable to cope with the pressures and excesses of mankind.

The Galapagos penguin lives on the Equator, off the coast of Ecuador. The islands of the south Atlantic, including the Falklands and the South Orkneys, hold colonies of chinstraps, rockhoppers, and gentoos, as well as other species of penguins.

The breeding assemblies can be enormous, with millions of birds jammed into barren hillsides above the sea. The blue penguin, on the other hand, nests in burrows it digs (or from which it chases nesting shearwaters), coming out only at night, to the delight of penguin-watchers who gather to view the spectacle under floodlights.

🐦3🐦

COURTSHIP AND NESTING

There is only one universal in the breeding behavior of birds: all of them lay eggs. Beyond that, anything goes. Courtship and nesting rituals range from the exquisite to the simply ridiculous and the bizarre—at least to human eyes. In every case, the birds are doing what works to attract a mate and raise another generation.

♦ ♦ ♦

Posted: No Trespassing

The first order of business is setting up a territory and attracting a mate. Birds use their bright colors, specialized feathers, songs, calls, or a combination of everything to find the opposite sex and scare off rivals. The scarlet wing patches of a male red-winged blackbird are badges used to indicate social status, and are flashed at intruding males that must then retreat or fight. A male whose epaulets are dyed black will lose his territory almost immediately.

Attracting a Mate

The woodcock is a rather dumpy, cryptically colored shorebird that is all but invisible against the forest floor, where it hunts for worms. But in the springtime the males gather on traditional leks (courting grounds), where females will come to find a mate.

As the sun sets in March, April, and May, the male woodcock begins to sing: he rears upright, long beak pointed down, and gives a nasal *peent!* The call sounds more like a frog than a bird, and is repeated every couple of seconds for several minutes. Then the male launches himself into the air, where he is just visible against the twilight sky. He spirals upward over the lek with a high-pitched twittering noise caused by specially modified primary feathers on his wings, which whistle as they are flapped. At the peak of his spiral, a hundred or more feet above the ground, he suddenly stops flapping and tumbles, headlong, to earth. The wing feathers are now silent, and the woodcock gives a vocal gurgle that sounds like water running from a bottle. Scant yards above the ground he opens his wings and stops his plummet, landing gently near his original position to resume "peenting."

Love on the Lek

Many birds use leks to increase the chances of males and females finding each other. One is the ruff, a European shorebird often found in small numbers along the East Coast. Males have an outlandish combination of a wide ruff of neck feathers (hence the name) and two bulbous ear tufts of feathers. At rest, the male's adornments lie flat, but when a female arrives, muscles pull the feathers erect. Furthermore, each male is colored differently—one may have a black ruff with chestnut ear tufts; another's head ornaments may be all white; others may carry ruffs of purple, cream or russet; and the ruffs may be plain, striped, or barred.

The American coot's breeding display is low-key; the male swims after the female, raising his wingtips and lowering his head, then showing off his white undertail feathers—the only flashy bit of plumage it has to offer.

The female, or reeve, is a plain mix of buff and white, with no ruff or ear tufts. Her arrival on the lek sets off a flurry of displaying and fights among the males. Once mated (and she may mate with several males in quick succession) the reeve goes off to nest and raise her young alone, without male assistance.

In the United States and Canada, the birds best known for leks and courtship displays are members of the grouse family, particularly sharp-tailed grouse, sage grouse, and prairie chickens. Male prairie chickens have inflatable air sacs on either side of the neck—yellow in the greater prairie chicken, orange-red in the rare lesser prairie chicken. When displaying, the males inflate the sacs, raise a set of long, dark neck feathers over their heads and make a deep booming sound as air is forced from the sacs. The sharp-tailed grouse has small, purple air sacs, but the key to its courtship display is a dance of stamping feet, raised tail, and spread wings—a dance that several groups of Native Americans from the plains states copied for themselves.

The big sage grouse of the western Plains has twin air sacs, which droop down over both sides of the breast and are covered in white feathers, looking vaguely like a life jacket. When courting in early spring, the males inflate the yellow sacs, fan their pointy, brown tails and make a rapid popping noise as the sacs deflate.

Generally, the dominant male grouse get the spot nearest the center of the lek, where most of the females congregate. In some cases, one or two top males will sire virtually all the young hatched from a spring's matings.

Bower Builders

Ruffs and sage grouse simply pick an open area for a lek. But for one family of Australian and New Guinean birds, that isn't good enough.

The bowerbirds go to elaborate lengths to create the perfect environment for courtship. To attract a mate they rely on construction skills rather than on impressive plumage, like their close relatives the birds of paradise. The crestless bowerbird starts by picking a tree in a small clearing. Making thousands of trips for materials, the male piles small twigs and sticks against the tree, eventually forming a conically roofed hut that may be 6 feet high, with a low entrance and a wide, encircling wall that forms a courtyard. Here he arranges flowers, seashells, brightly colored berries, and small bits of human debris that catch his eye.

The satin bowerbird of Australia takes a different approach. He lays a floor of close-fitting twigs in an area about 4 feet wide, then jams sticks into the flooring to create two parallel walls about a foot long, which are always oriented north to south. Once the frame is done, the male turns to painting. He chews up berries, charcoal, or fruit to make a bluish mash, then slathers the "paint" onto the bower with wads of shredded bark—one of the very few instances of the use of tools by an animal. To complete the job, the satin bowerbird collects any small blue object he can find—flowers; shells; bits of glass, plastic, or paper; berries. Some of the decorations are scavenged from the landscape, but satin bowerbirds have a highly developed sense of larceny, and steal freely from each other. The collec-

Flight plays a very important role in the courtship displays of most birds of prey. Among the red-tailed hawks, the pair will circle close together, the male above the female, or he may spiral high above her, then drop into a spectacular swooping dive, which she meets, locking her talons with his momentarily. He may also deliver food to her—an act common among birds.

tions can be huge; one male Lauterbach's bowerbird had accumulated more than eleven pounds of pale pebbles.

Ironically, despite the males' obvious construction skills, he lends his eventual mate no assistance with the nest, which she must build herself.

Attention Grabber

Anything to attract attention. The male blue bird of paradise in New Guinea hangs upside down from a branch, allowing his flimsy blue flank feathers to fan out gloriously. Then he swings slowly from side to side, all the while singing in a monotone.

Thanks to nature specials on television, many people have seen the courtship displays of the albatross family. The wandering albatross, for instance, faces its mate with its 12-foot wings extended; the mate does the same, and both birds point their bills skyward. Other steps in the mating process (not all of which are performed by all albatross species) include bowing to each other, clacking their bills together, walking in synchronization while swaying from side to side, and feeding each other regurgitated food.

Flight plays an important role in the displays of many birds. Birds of prey in particular display in the air, swooping, rolling, and diving for the benefit of an admiring mate, sometimes locking talons in midair. The northern harrier, or marsh hawk, gives a complicated display over the prairies and grasslands of North America, in which the male performs a series of rolling loops, like the coils of a stretched spring. He also transfers food—mice and small birds—to the female while both are airborne.

In some areas this ritual disappeared in the 1960s, when harrier populations suffered the ravages of the pesticide DDT. It was apparently a learned, rather than instinctive, behavior, and with older males gone the youngsters had few adults to teach them. Fortunately harriers are again sky-dancing, although it took twenty years for the ritual to become reestablished.

Swifts, which spend almost every waking minute on the wing, not surprisingly mate there. White-throated swifts of the American West copulate high in the air, and drift earthward on

fluttering wings before breaking off just a few feet above the ground.

The western grebe has a complicated courtship display that involves a beautifully choreographed dance. The two grebes, side-by-side with necks arched, race furiously across the surface of the water. The birds also present each other with bits of aquatic plants.

Angling for Best Effect

Because his iridescent throat gorget and head feathers must be seen at the right angle to shine their best, the male Anna's hummingbird takes the relative position of the sun and his prospective mate into account before starting his display flight. Thus once in the air doing spectacular looping dives, the male glows with a vivid rose-red when seen from the female's perspective.

The Arctic Flasher

The buff-breasted sandpiper of the North American arctic is a flasher; a male will flash open his pale wings toward approaching females, which will spend several minutes examining his mottled wing linings. Sometimes as many as a half-dozen females will crowd around a single male before leaving, en masse, to go check out a nearby competitor.

Exceptional Phalaropes

With birds, it seems, there is an exception to every rule, and so it is with the phalaropes, which set courtship convention on its head.

The California quail has no true song, but a variety of calls for flock communication, including a loud *Chi-ca-go!* that helps keep the birds together. California quail form large flocks in the winter, sometimes numbering 200 individuals. The flocks break up with the coming of spring.

There are three species of these tiny shorebirds in North America: the Wilson's, the red, and the red-necked. Wilson's breeds in the Great Lakes region and much of the West, while the other two are arctic breeders. All three exhibit sexual role reversal. The females are the more colorful of the pair, with rich tones of red, buff, and gray, depending on the species, while the males are somewhat drabber. The females initiate courtship; among the Wilson's phalarope she chases the male through the air, or swims up to him while expanding her neck feathers and giving a croaking sound.

While the female may choose the site for the nest and indicate it with a shallow scrape, it is the male who lines the nest, and after the four eggs are laid, it is the male who incubates them for three weeks, keeping them warm with a brood patch that in other birds is found on the females. The male gets no help in raising the chicks, either, although young birds can walk and feed themselves from birth.

Other birds that exhibit role reversal include the painted snipe of Europe, the cassowary of Australia, and the northern jaçana of the American tropics.

Songs of Love

Sound can be as important as sight in courtship, which is why birds are the world's best songsters. A male's tune serves as an advertisement for a mate and an auditory "No Trespassing" sign for others of his species, but usually has no effect on other species of birds.

Generally speaking, bird vocalizations comes in two varieties: calls and songs. Calls are short and simple, and usually have to do with flocking or some other social, but nonbreeding, behavior; a good example are the

39

Birdsong, while a delight to human ears, has serious purposes—mate attraction and territorial defense. Most species have unique songs, but the brown thrasher (top left) and gray catbird (center) are mimics. This plate, from Alexander Wilson's landmark *American Ornithology,* also shows four warblers, two of which Wilson identified as thrushes.

"chuckle" calls of robins as they settle in for the evening roost. Another variation are alarm calls, like the sharp *chip!* of a disturbed cardinal. Both sexes ordinarily give calls.

Songs are usually richer, more complex, and exclusively male. For most songbirds, singing takes the place of physical aggression, although an intruder who does not heed the verbal "fence" of song will be routed by force. There are other advantages as well. A song can be heard despite thick cover, or in bad weather, and as soon as the singer stops, a predator will have a harder time zeroing in on it.

Just as people from different regions may speak the same language with different accents and dialects, some birds also have distinct dialects. The call of a song sparrow in Alaska is subtly different from that of a song sparrow in Virginia or Maine, even though all three are sufficiently similar to be recognizable as song sparrow tunes. While the basic theme appears to be instinctive, the regional variations are learned from neighboring males when the bird is very young.

Most birds have an instinctive song that all males of their species sing, but the three members of the family *Mimidae* pick and choose from what they hear around them.

The best-known of these mimics is the northern mockingbird, renowned for its impersonations. Within ten or fifteen minutes, a male mockingbird may sing snatches of songs from more than two dozen other birds—not to mention original phrases of its own and imitations of barking dogs, police sirens, lifeguard whistles, and whatever other repetitive noises might have caught the bird's fancy. Scientists have shown that female mockingbirds are attracted to the males with the widest range of songs, thus providing an evolutionary incentive for males to appropriate lots of stolen tunes.

There are several other mimics in North America; two, the gray catbird and the brown thrasher, are relatives of the mockingbird. The catbird repeats each swiped phrase only once, and intersperses lots of catlike "mew" notes through its song. The thrasher sings each phrase two or three times, making it possible to identify the singer even though it is hidden.

The European starling can also produce realistic imitations of other bird calls, as can the yellow-breasted chat, a large warbler of brush and thickets. And while it might not be a case of mimicry, the blue jay has a call that is astonishingly close to the long, descending whistle of the red-shouldered hawk. A breeding burrowing owl, threatened in its underground nest, gives a harsh, buzzing sound that closely matches that of an angry prairie rattlesnake. Few predators linger long enough to discover the truth.

Many kinds of sound play a role in courtship. Male woodpeckers do not sing well, so they use their heads, quite literally, to get the message out. They drum rapidly on hollow logs and tree limbs, filling the woods with a staccato rumbling. They are attracted to any surface that resonates, which is why woodpeckers in the spring often drum on aluminum shed roofs and even the hoods of cars, much to the annoyance of the human owners.

Woodpecker bills perform double-duty, both as food-gathering tools and courtship instruments. Woodpeckers—in this case pileated, ivory-billed, and red-headed, by Wilson—drum rapidly on hollow logs and branches to attract a mate; birders can identify each species by its rhythm.

A Virginia rail carefully turns its eggs, hidden in a low-lying nest built among the thick reeds of a freshwater marsh. Bird nests run the gamut from dirt scratches to complex structures but most are simple grass bowls like the rail's.

The male ruffed grouse does not vocalize in the spring, but instead mounts a fallen log or prominent rock in the woods. Standing upright, he flares his tail and his crest, then begins to beat his wings against the air: *Thump . . . thump . . . thump thump thumpthumpthumpthump.* The drumming starts slowly and quickly builds, something like the sound of a motorcycle engine kicking over and then cutting out. It is very low-pitched—so low, in fact, that great horned owls, which share the oak forests with the grouse, cannot detect it.

Nesting

Nests run the gamut from none (the common murre simply lays its single egg on a bare cliff ledge high above the sea) to the elaborate. The Old World weavers are perhaps the most accomplished nest builders of all. Some, like the introduced house sparrow so common around human habitation in North America, build fairly simple domed nests of twigs, grass, and junk. At the other extreme is the hanging nest of the baya weaver of Southeast Asia, intricately woven of grass to form

Common murres nest on sheer cliffs high above the North Atlantic, each pair laying a single egg on the bare rocks. The murre's sharply pointed egg was once thought to be less likely to roll off the edge than a rounder shape; biologists later realized that the ledges favored by murres are so narrow that almost any egg, if carelessly bumped, will tumble over the side.

a gourd-shaped nest suspended from a long woven tube. Inside the gourd portion are two chambers: a lower one for the eggs, and an upper chamber that curves into an entrance tube that hangs down like an elephant's trunk. In all, the nest may be more than 2 feet long.

The social weavers of South Africa employ the same building skills, but on a cooperative scale. As many as 300 pairs may work together to assemble a thatched straw roof in the branches of a tree. Once the waterproof ceiling is finished, each pair builds its own hanging nest beneath, jammed close to each other in the drooping straw. The result is a veritable apartment building for birds, with some nests as large as 10 feet by 15 feet.

In the New World, members of the blackbird family are the most skillful nest builders. One is the northern (formerly Baltimore) oriole, whose pendulous nest of grass, twine, and weed fibers is a familiar sight in shade trees. Further south, the oropendolas of the Central American tropics build outsized hanging nests, carefully interlocking long strands of grass to form pockets nearly 6 feet long.

The fairy tern of the tropical Pacific lays but a single egg, and it does so in the most unlikely of places—on the bare branch of a tree. The egg is balanced perfectly on the bark, undisturbed by the incubating parent. One subspecies goes even further out on a limb, laying its egg on the fragile leaflets of the coconut palm. Substitutions of human manufacture are accepted, like the vertical water valve that cup ported a tern egg in its metal cup.

To most people, the nest of the American robin is the quintessential bird nest. The construction is done mostly by the female, who starts with a layer of mud to anchor the nest to the crotch of a tree. For several days she will add to it with grass and weed fibers, mixing in more mud to serve as mortar, frequently checking the fit by sitting in the growing cup and molding it to her body. The final touch is a lining of fine grasses to cushion the eggs. The nest may sit empty for as long as two weeks before she starts laying her clutch, on average one egg per day, usually in the early morning. Only when the clutch is complete will she begin incubating.

For some birds, nest security means going underground. The bank swallow (known as the sand martin in Europe) forms large colonies wherever the birds find a steep bank of soft, rock-free soil; many colonies are on eroded riverbanks, and along roads. The swallows dig their own burrows, which extend as much as 4 feet into the soil, culminating in a small, round chamber lined with feathers and grass.

The belted kingfisher looks for the same kind of waterside banks as the bank swallow, but nests alone rather than in colonies. The deep burrow is used year after year, and eventually acquires a thick flooring of fish scales and bones from the regurgitated food pellets of previous occupants.

An emperor penguin, nesting in the bitter cold of the Antarctic winter when temperatures plummet to -70 degrees, cannot allow its egg to touch the ground, so a nest is out of the question. Thus, when the females lays the single, green white egg, she transfers it from her warm feet to those of her mate, who tucks it up into a special flap of belly skin to keep it warm. Then she heads out cross-country for open water, to replace the large percentage of body fat she lost during the courtship cycle.

The male, meanwhile, hunkers down for the duration. Although he can shuffle about slowly, for the most part he sits still, enduring the hideous cold and perpetual darkness of winter. For more than two months the male penguin sits quietly, without eating, carefully incubating the egg that rests on his feet. He loses nearly half of his body weight, dropping to an emaciated 50 to 55 pounds, yet when the chick hatches he must secrete a nourishing liquid from his throat on which to feed it. Fortunately, his mate usually returns at just about that time, allowing the male to go to sea for a well-deserved meal—his first in nearly four months.

Almost every conceivable building material finds its way into a bird's nest somewhere. Great-crested flycatchers use shed snakeskins, ferruginous hawks decorate their nests with dried horse dung, ruby-throated hummingbirds use plant down (the fluffy fibers of milkweed and thistle seeds, for instance), spider webs, and lichen. The gabar goshawk of Africa collects live spiders and their webs, so that the cobweb coating of its nest is constantly renewed. Rocks and seashells are common nest ornaments for shorebirds, while cliff swallows use pellets of mud to make their jug-shaped nests.

Glued in Place

The strangest building material of all is that of the edible swiftlet, an Asian species that builds a small, half-circular cup from strands of its own dried saliva (the nest is the main ingredient in bird's-nest soup). In the United States, the chimney swift uses its sticky saliva to glue twigs to each other and to the wall of the chimney or silo in which the bird is nesting.

Another swift with an odd nest is the African palm swift, which uses saliva to glue a thumb-sized pad of feathers to the outermost end of a palm leaf. To the feathers are glued her two eggs— both standing upright—which the swift incubates by clinging to the wildly swaying palm frond for two weeks.

When the chicks hatch, they instinctively grip the feather pad for dear life until they are old enough to fly.

Life After Death

Biologists aren't joking when they say that dead wood is alive—especially from the standpoint of birds. In North America, 78 species are either partly or wholly reliant on cavities in trees, usually dead ones. Some, like the woodpeckers, nuthatches, and chickadees, excavate their own holes, but many other birds use hand-me-down nests originally cut by another owner, or naturally made. Most are songbirds, but there are cavity-nesting waterfowl (wood ducks, mergansers, buffleheads, goldeneyes, and whistling-ducks) and raptors (American kestrels and a number of owls).

Unfortunately, dead wood is often viewed as waste by foresters and landowners, who cut it for firewood or to "clean up" a woodland. But ecologically, dead wood can be one of the most valuable resources a forest holds.

Hornbills: Doing Time

A female bird, sitting patiently on her eggs for weeks at a time while the embryos develop, may appear trapped by life. But the female great hornbill of Africa is trapped in reality.

Great hornbills are huge birds, nearly 5 feet long, with massive, toucanlike bills and horny shields rising over their foreheads. They nest in hollow trees, but a hole big enough to admit a hornbill would also be large enough to admit a monkey or some other egg-stealing predator. So when the female hornbill is about to lay her eggs, she and her mate work to seal up the opening—with her inside. Using a plaster-like mix of mud, stomach secretions, and dung, the hornbills close the hole, leaving just a thin slit through which the male can pass food to his mate. Other hornbills species follow the same procedure.

Inside, the female lays and incubates her eggs, and after the three or four chicks hatch she takes food from the male and feeds them. So it goes for weeks on end—up to 12 weeks in some hornbill species. Finally the plaster is chipped away and the female is released, although the young may reseal the opening for a few more weeks until they reach full size.

Cities offer cold comfort to most birds, but the peregrine falcon, which nests on cliffs in the wild, has taken to skyscraper ledges and large bridges as an urban substitute.

Megapodes

Birds, being warm-blooded, keep their eggs warm and viable by incubating them close to their bodies, unlike cold-blooded reptiles that must rely on the warmth of the sun or rotting vegetation to incubate their eggs. One group of birds, however, takes the reptilian approach.

The megapodes are turkeylike fowl of Australia, the Philippines, and several nearby islands. All use external heat to warm their eggs, like the maleo fowl, which migrates from the shady jungles to the sunny beaches, where it buries its clutch in black, sun-warmed volcanic sand. Those megapodes that live in damp, humid climates heap rotting vegetation over their eggs. The most ambitious of the lot is the mallee fowl of Aus-

tralia, which lives in semidesert where decomposition won't provide enough heat, and so must work with the sun to raise a family.

Starting four months before the first egg is laid, the male digs a wide pit in the soil, then builds on it a huge mound of rotting vegetation covered with a layer of sand, 15 to 20 feet wide and several feet high. In this mound are buried the female's eggs, each in its own chamber, which are kept at an even 92 degrees by the decompositional heat of the leaves and mulch around them, and the warmth of the sun on the sand above. To maintain a constant temperature, the male mallee fowl tests the mound by sticking his beak into the

Species	Clutch size (range)	Incubation (days)
CLUTCH SIZE AND INCUBATION		
Canada goose	4–7	25
Mallard	8–15	25–30
Killdeer	3–5	25–28
California gull	3–5	25–29
California condor	1	45–50
Bald eagle	1–3	35
Red-tailed hawk	1–3	30–35
American kestrel	4–7	30
Northern bobwhite	5–28	22
Mourning dove	2	14
Great horned owl	1–4	31
Black-chinned hummingbird	2	14
Barn swallow	3–7	15
Eastern bluebird	4–6	12–14
American robin	3–8	12–14
Red-eyed vireo	4	12–14
Yellow warbler	4–5	11–12
Common yellowthroat	4	11–12
Northern cardinal	2–5	12–14
Song sparrow	3–4	12–14

top and picking up some mulch in his mouth; temperature-sensitive nerves in his tongue tell him if it is too cool (in which case he piles on more sand and debris) or too hot (in which case he scratches away at the mound, opening up a crater at the top).

This incessant test-and-scratch routine goes on for eight weeks, among the longest incubation periods of any bird species. The young are highly developed at hatching, capable of caring for themselves; this is fortunate, because the parents, having expended more than ten months in nest preparation and care, pay the chicks no heed at all.

Altricial or Precocial?

Baby birds come in two types: altricial and precocial. Altricial chicks, born helpless, blind, and almost naked, include virtually all of the songbirds, which can barely hold up their heads at birth. Precocial young, on the other hand, come out of the egg covered in protective down, with eyes open and capable of walking, swimming, and feeding themselves. Gamebirds, shorebirds, and waterfowl all have precocial young.

There are, of course, intergrades. Common loon chicks are considered semiprecocial; they are alert and mobile, but remain in the nest for a few days to be fed. Buteos (soaring hawks like red-tails) are semialtricial, hatched with down and open eyes, but unable to leave the nest for several weeks. Falcons are even less developed at hatching, with closed eyes and weak necks.

Generally speaking, the incubation time for eggs of altricial species is

Bald eagles, like many birds of prey, usually lay more than one egg, but often only raise a single chick to maturity. In what is known as the "Cain and Abel syndrome," the older (and larger) chick often kills its weaker sibling. This Maine eagle nest, with two eaglets ready to fly, was a lucky exception, perhaps because abundant food kept competition and aggression to a minimum.

shorter than that for precocial species, which makes sense considering the greater degree of prenatal development needed for precocial young.

"Cain and Abel" Eagles

The "Cain and Abel syndrome," named for the Biblical murderer and his victim, is common in many large raptors. Golden eagles, for instance, routinely lay two eggs. Because the female begins incubating as soon as the first egg is laid (rather than waiting for a complete clutch, as smaller birds do), the eggs hatch in sequence, with one sibling inevitably much bigger than the other. The older sibling very often kills (and sometimes eats) the younger before they fledge, usually through direct attack but also by hogging the food and constantly harassing the smaller eaglet. While this appears cruel and wasteful, having two chicks is actually an insurance policy for the species, providing a back-up chick should something happen to the other.

Nest Parasitism

The brown-headed cowbird evolved on the prairies of North America, following the herds of bison on their epic migrations, feeding on the insects the great beasts would stir up. Unfortunately, the bison herds didn't stop conveniently during the breeding season, which left the cowbirds in a quandary. They could not raise chicks on the move, but to stop for more than a month would mean being left behind by the bison—and their food supply.

The cowbird solved the problem by becoming a nest parasite. When the female is ready to lay an egg she seeks out the nest of another small passerine like a finch or a warbler, tosses out the owner's eggs and lays her own in its place. Even though the cowbird egg is larger and differently colored than the host's, many parasitized birds do not seem to notice the switch, and incubate the intruder as if it were their own. The baby cowbird grows rapidly, quickly eclipsing the size of its foster parents; it is tragically comic to see a tiny song sparrow stuffing the mouth of a cowbird chick nearly twice its size.

Not all birds fall for the ruse. Yellow warblers, which are common cowbird hosts, will build a new nest layer right over top of the substituted eggs, and as many as five extra layers have been found in the nest of a single persistent warbler. Others, like robins, will recognize the cowbird egg as something foreign, and simply toss it out of the nest.

Cowbirds were originally confined to the Plains, but when humans cut the Eastern forests they opened new realms for the cowbird, which easily switched from bison to cows. Many eastern bird species had no experience with cowbird parasitism, and some biologists blame the cowbird, at least in part, for declines of forest-dwelling species like thrushes, vireos, and some warblers. Cowbird parasitism of the endangered Kirtland's warbler in Michigan became so bad that biologists trapped and removed thousands of cowbirds from the warbler's restricted nesting range.

The European cuckoo has a more refined approach to nest parasitism than the cowbird. Cuckoos from different regions of Europe specialize in different host species, and their eggs mimic those of the hosts. In areas where brambling are the major host species the cuckoo's eggs are greenish with dark spots like the brambling's, while those that parasitize great reed warblers match their host's white, blotched eggs. The female will remove the host's eggs before laying her one egg, but in case the host lays more, the newly hatched cuckoo chick has an instinctive reaction that eliminates competition. Blind and naked, it will nevertheless automati-

(Box continues on next page)

cally push against anything touching its back. If that something is another egg, the baby cuckoo will push it out of the nest. Such nest parasitism is not practiced by the two U.S. cuckoo species, the black-billed and yellow-billed, which raise their own young.

A more brutal approach is taken by the African honey-guides. A honey-guide nestling is hatched with two wickedly curving hooks at the end of the beak, which it uses against its foster nestmates, killing them. By the time the honey-guide chick is two weeks old—and by then an only child—the hooks drop off.

Egg Colors

The color of birds' eggs are almost as varied as the plumage of the birds themselves. While plain white is common, especially for those that nest in tree cavities or burrows, almost every other hue can be found on a bird egg somewhere or other.

The pigment is applied during the egg's final passage down the oviduct and uterus. The color may be a uniform tone, like the smooth blue-green of a robin's egg, or it may be applied in random spots, scrawls, and blotches as the egg twists through the oviduct and past the pigment cells. In some birds the first eggs of a clutch are the most heavily marked, indicating that the pigment cells may run dry toward the end.

Emus and cassowaries lay dark greenish eggs with textured, pebbly shells. The tinamous of South America, on the other hand, lay eggs so smooth and shiny that they appear to have been varnished. Among North American birds, the sharp-shinned hawk's chestnut-blotched eggs were once prized by oologists, or egg collectors, who in the nineteenth century amassed enormous collections of blown eggs, much to the detriment of the birds. Such collecting of eggs is today illegal except for scientific study.

Waterlogged Parents

At the other end of the scale from the nest parasites, which dump their kids off on someone else, is the Namaqua sandgrouse of the Kalahari Desert. Although it nests in an arid environment, the sandgrouse's chicks must have water each day. In some species the adults regurgitate it along with food, but the Namaqua sandgrouse has a different method of watering its young.

Each day the male flies as much as a hundred miles to a watering hole, where he wades out, belly deep, and slowly rocks back and forth with his breast feathers fluffed out. Special belly feathers absorb many times their weight in water, and store it safely while the sandgrouse laboriously flies all the way back to the nest. By nibbling at the feathers (birds have no lips, so they cannot suck) the chicks get their daily drink—a routine that may go on for seven weeks, until they are fledged and can make the trip themselves.

A Happy Ending

A bird with a deformity or injury may not be accepted, even by its mate. Such was the case with two ringed plovers, common European shorebirds, which had each lost a leg between one mating season and the next in the 1930s. Because the birds were banded, researchers could tell that both crippled birds were rejected by their former mates. But this story had a happy ending. The two injured birds were of opposite sexes; they met, mated, and raised a brood of young. True love—or the bird equivalent—conquers again.

♦ ♦ ♦

4

FOOD AND FEEDING

Just as birds have evolved to fill almost every habitat on Earth, so too have they developed wide-ranging tastes. If something is even remotely edible, it's a good bet that some bird eats it.

How a bird gets its food can be just as interesting as what it eats. For an herbivorous species, eating may be a fairly straightforward affair: find a fruit tree and dig in. But for predators the game is far more complex, involving chase, capture, and avoidance. Whether their meals are vegetable or animal, birds also fit into the larger scheme of life, the intricate interrelationships known as the food web.

Incidentally, to say that a bird "eats like a bird" is far from the mark. Birds, with their high metabolisms and body temperatures, actually need more food than many other creatures. A human with the metabolism of a hummingbird would have to eat 1½ times his or her weight in food every day.

◆ ◆ ◆

Beak Specialties

A bird's beak is a marvelously pliable tool, prone to evolutionary tinkering, usually for the sake of eating. A scientist who has never seen a species of bird before can make some educated guesses about its lifestyle based solely on its bill, just as a mammalogist can surmise a mammal's life from its teeth.

A seed-eating bird, which must crack the tough shells to get to the germ inside, needs a heavy, crushing beak—the sort carried by cardinals, grosbeaks, and buntings. Sparrows, which on the whole eat finer weed seeds that don't require such extreme pressure to open, have finer, thinner bills. Cross-

53

An immature red-shouldered hawk swoops into a covey of bobwhite, in one of Audubon's most dramatic works. Actually, red-shouldereds largely eat small mammals, insects, reptiles, and amphibians—a fact known to Audubon, who painted another specimen holding a dead bullfrog.

bills—finches that live in the boreal forests and feed on the seeds of conifer trees—have specialized bills with thin, overlapping tips to deftly pry open stubborn cone scales.

Warblers and other insect-eaters have thin, pointed bills perfect for extracting bugs from beneath leaves and from the cracks between bark; those like the brown creeper, which specialize in bark probing, often have downward-curved bills for greater efficiency. Chickadees and titmice, which feed on insects in the summer but add seeds to their diet in the winter (along with dormant bugs) have an intermediate beak. A chickadee's bill is not strong enough to crack a sunflower seed, however, so the bird carries the seed off in its beak, perches, then grips the seed beneath its feet and hammers it open with its bill.

Larger birds have beak specializations for hunting. The beak of a peregrine falcon (as well as the other falcons) has a peculiar notch along the lower edge of the upper mandible that fits nicely between the neck vertebrae of the birds the peregrine hunts. Should the quarry not be killed in the peregrine's lightning-bolt attack, the hawk can quickly slice the spinal cord, instantly killing the smaller bird.

The herons and egrets have long, swordlike bills used for catching fish, reptiles, and amphibians, but the birds don't usually spear their prey; in fact, a heron that accidentally skewers a fish may spend several minutes looking befuddled, trying to figure out how to get the blasted thing off. The anhinga, however, does use its bill as a spear. Also known as the water turkey, this cormorantlike bird dives with ease, stalking bluegills and other small fish. Once it has speared a meal the anhinga surfaces, tosses the fish into the air and grabs it with its open bill, swallowing it head first.

A woodpecker's bill, although the most obvious tool, is only part of its wood-boring equipment. Thick and chisel-shaped, the bill of a pileated woodpecker, the largest common North American species, is about 3 inches long. Powered by strong blows of the head (which is protected by a thick, shock-absorbing skull), the beak easily cuts through pine and oak to reveal the tunnels of carpenter ants, the woodpecker's main food. Once exposed, the ants are zapped with the bird's barbed tongue. The tongue of the pileated—indeed of all woodpeckers—is extremely long; in some species the hyoid bone at the base of the tongue actually splits to either side of the neck and wraps up and back, around the bird's skull to anchor in its right nostril—thus giving the tongue even greater length.

A Side Order of Feathers

Grebes routinely eat their own feathers, often in large quantities, and also feed feathers to their chicks. The reason seems to be as protection for the stomach against the sharp bones of fish, which make up most of the rest of the grebe's diet.

A pair of evening grosbeaks nonchalantly crack sunflower seeds with their heavy bills. Like most seed-eating birds, the grosbeaks switch to a diet heavy on insects in the summertime, and their chicks, which require protein while growing, are fed almost nothing but bugs.

BIRD DIETS

Some dietary specializations among North America's birds (these usually do not reflect the species' entire diet):

Storm-petrel: floating oil from dead marine mammals

Black-necked stilt: brine flies

Wilson's phalarope: insects swirled to surface as bird spins rapidly in water

American woodcock: earthworms, almost exclusively

Mississippi kite: large insects

Snail kite: *Pomacea* snails, exclusively

Osprey: fish, almost exclusively

Spruce grouse: conifer buds and needles

Sage grouse: sagebrush leaves

Band-tailed pigeon: acorns

Groove-billed ani: parasitic insects on cattle

Elf owl: scorpions

Northern flicker: ants

Yellow-bellied sapsucker: tree sap, inner bark

Acorn woodpecker: acorns, other nuts stored in communal hordes

Ivory-billed woodpecker: larvae of wood-boring beetles, almost exclusively

Golden-crowned kinglet: tree sap, often from sapsucker borings

Northern shrike: mice, birds, large insects

American dipper: insects caught by swimming along stream bottoms

Northern oriole: flower nectar

Red and **white-winged crossbills:** conifer seeds, pried free with crossed beaks

A Bloated Carcass to Go, Please

Vultures are certainly the bird world's least delicate eaters, although human revulsion at their food masks the vital job they do in keeping the outdoors clean, especially in hot regions like Africa that support great numbers of large mammals. Still, there's no rush to set up vulture-feeding stations the way folks put out sunflower seed.

The Old World, particularly Africa, has far more vultures than the New World. North America, for instance, has only three: the turkey and black vultures, and the endangered California condor. The fossil record shows that there once were quite a few more species of scavengers, especially during the Pleistocene Epoch, when the continent held immense herds of native camels, horses, long-horned bison, mastodons, and other gigantic grazers. But ten thousand years ago most of those species became extinct, for reasons still not clearly understood. Many of the large vultures died out with them, and the range of the California condor shrank from continent-wide to just the West Coast where humans all but sealed its fate.

A vulture's naked head is an adaptation for its feeding habits; bare skin is easier to clean than feathers, which would become matted with blood and gore. A vulture or condor that has been reaching inside a carcass will carefully wipe its head clean on grass or sand, and will spend just as much time preening itself as does any other bird with a more pleasant diet.

The Egyptian vulture is found over

most of Africa, the Middle East, and southern Europe. It is an attractive bird, white with black wingtips, and just the front of its face showing bare, yellow skin. It is often the last bird to feed on a carcass, picking the bones after the larger vultures have finished with it, but in East Africa the Egyptian has developed a unique way of unlocking a food source all its own—the eggs of the ostrich.

Ostrich eggs are big and nutritious, but they also have very thick shells, which the small Egyptian vulture cannot crack with its bill. So the vulture will pick up small rocks and repeatedly throw them at the egg until it cracks— another rare instance of a bird using a tool.

The lammergeier, or bearded vulture of Africa and Eurasia, has a very specialized feeding practice—gleaning the large bones left over from the kills of carnivores like brown bears, wolves, and lions. The vulture carries the bones high into the air and drops them to the ground, smashing them to expose the nutritious marrow inside, although lammergeiers also eat some of the bone fragments themselves. Lammergeiers and a few other raptors have been known to drop turtles to the rocks; the ancient Greek poet Aeschylus was killed by such a falling turtle, dropped by an eagle.

Water, Water Everywhere

The group of birds called tubenoses includes the shearwaters and petrels, birds that spend the majority of their life at sea. Like all living things they require moisture, but fresh water is im-

Black vultures, like these by Audubon, depend largely on sight to locate carrion, while the turkey vulture uses both vision and its unusually keen—for a bird—sense of smell to find food. As Audubon correctly showed, scavenging birds often treat the eyes as a special delicacy.

A Forster's tern watches for the telltale ripple of minnows at the water's surface; it will then plunge headfirst into the water. A tern may dive a dozen times before finally coming up with a fish, and a pair with several young in the nest to feed may make hundreds of strikes in the course of a day, trying to fill the hungry mouths.

possible to find in the middle of the ocean. So tubenoses can drink saltwater.

For most vertebrates that would be fatal in short order, because ocean water is three times saltier than an animal's body fluids, and it would require more moisture to excrete the salt than the drink would have provided; this is why shipwrecked sailors who drink seawater can die of dehydration. But the tubenoses have special nasal glands around the eyes that process the blood and remove the salt, which is ejected through the tubular nostrils.

Other seabirds that have salt glands, include gulls, puffins, and oceanic ducks such as eiders. Interestingly, ducks that usually live on freshwater, such as mallards, will develop enlarged salt glands if they move to a marine environment, as some do when they fly to winter quarters along the coast.

Gone Fishing

Most of a bird's hunting techniques are instinctive, but occasionally a species will show a capacity for learning a new trick. One such is the green-backed heron, a common wading bird over most of the United States and Canada. In a few scattered locations, green-backeds have discovered that if they drop small bits of bread—gleaned from nearby picnic grounds—into the water, minnows will rise to the bait. Because green-backed herons eat minnows, this obviously works out nicely from the bird's perspective.

Food Far and Near

When a woodcock is probing the damp earth for worms, it will sometimes stamp its feet sharply on the ground,

Common barn owls are among the most nocturnal of birds, doing virtually all of their hunting after full darkness has arrived. They have large, highly sensitive eyes, soft flight feathers to muffle sound, and superb hearing, accentuated by their round facial disks, for finding mice.

apparently to stir the worms into moving. The trick may have something in common with the backwoods technique of driving a notched stick into the ground and "calling" worms to the surface by running another stick rapidly over the notches, sending vibrations through the soil. Regardless, the woodcock usually finds plenty to eat, and within a single 24-hour period may eat its weight (about 7 ounces) in worms.

Listening for Supper

Barn owls are among the most nocturnal of all the owls, and so are the most highly adapted to hunting in the dark. Their night vision is excellent, but what a mouse has to fear most is a barn owl's ears.

Biologists long knew that owls could catch mice in near-total darkness, but they were unsure of how the owls did it. Did they rely on hearing or vision? To find out, barn owls were placed in light-tight rooms and mice were released with them. Despite the total lack of light, the owls killed the mice. This suggested hearing, but there was also the possibility that the owls were using a form of infrared vision to spot the rodents' body heat. So more mice were released in the rooms; this time each had a ball of paper tied to its tail with a length of string.

The owls attacked the paper, which made more noise, thus proving that barn owls hunt by sound. More sophisticated research has shown that a barn owl's hearing system—the ears and the wide, round facial discs around the eyes—is one of the most sensitive in the animal world. In fact, even when the owl can see its prey, it apparently relies more on information from its ears than its eyes when coordinating an attack—a situation difficult for sight-oriented humans to comprehend.

Cooperative Honey Hunting

The black-throated honey-guide of Africa is a bird with a problem. It loves to eat bees and their honeycombs, but since the hives are usually underground or inside trees, the honey-guide can't reach them.

The bird solves its dilemma in a unique way. Over thousands of years it has developed a rapport with the ratel, or honey-badger, a weasel with a sweet tooth. When a honey-guide finds a hive, it goes in search of a ratel, and carefully leads it to the hive. Once the mammal has finished feeding on the honey and bee larvae, the bird moves in—not so much for the insects, as was originally thought, but for the beeswax, which it can partially digest thanks to special intestinal bacteria.

The honey-guides will also seek out people and show them the location of hives. In some parts of Africa it is believed to be bad luck not to leave some of the hive for the bird to enjoy.

A Little Roughage

As is known to every pigeon fancier or canary owner, some birds need grit in their diet. The fine gravel has no nutritional value, but in the bird's gizzard (a second, muscular stomach) the grit serves as a grinding medium to crush

Eastern screech-owls, like most owls, are dreadfully messy eaters, swallowing their prey whole or in large chunks. The fur, bones, and feathers are later regurgitated in a compact pellet, the analysis of which provides most of our information about owl food habits.

the seeds on which the bird feeds. Large birds need more grit; a turkey's gizzard may have as much as 2 ounces. Moas, the giant, flightless birds now extinct, swallowed gizzard stones that weighed as much as 5 pounds.

Penguins do not eat vegetable matter, and so would have no need for gizzard stones to aid digestion. But they swallow rocks anyway, apparently for ballast when swimming.

A bird's crop is an enlarged section of esophagus that serves as a storage pouch, allowing the bird to feed quickly and digest its meal later, in safety and leisure.

Pigeons and doves have a unique, double crop, however, that has two purposes. One part holds grain in the normal fashion, but the other produces "pigeon's milk," a secretion of the crop lining. The cheesy, high-protein substance is regurgitated to the young as soon as they hatch, and in some species is their sole food for the first five or six days; thereafter it is mixed with regurgitated grain.

Owls are messy eaters, often swallowing their prey whole, or tearing it into large chunks before gulping it down—bones, fur, organs, feathers, the works. The soft tissue is digestible, but the rest is not. Such roughage cannot pass through the entire digestive tract, so about eight hours after eating, the owls regurgitate a compact pellet of the fur, feathers, and bones. Because the pellets contain a very accurate record of everything the owl ate (even insect parts make it through unscathed), scientists rely on pellet analysis to learn about the birds' food habits.

Through pellet studies, we know that barn owls eat a preponderance of rodents—one study showed 78 percent mice and voles, 16 percent shrews, 4 percent moles, and 4 percent miscellaneous. Screech owls have broader tastes, and eat large insects, mice, small frogs, snakes, lizards, and a few songbirds.

Other birds also pass pellets, although the record they contain is not as complete as an owl's. Among them are gulls, crows, herons, hawks, and eagles. Flycatchers and other insect eaters pass tiny pellets of wing cases and bug legs, and kingfishers regurgitate pellets of scales and fish bones.

Specialist or Generalist?

Animals can be generalists or specialists when it comes to feeding. The great horned owl is an example of a generalist, eating whatever comes its way. At the fringe of a city, an owl may eat mostly rats, mice, and pigeons, while a great horned that hunts the wilderness of southern Canada would more likely take voles, snowshoe hares, and songbirds—as well as fish, reptiles, amphibians, large insects, and even carrion.

The snail kite of central Florida, on the other hand, is a specialist. It eats only one thing, apple snails of the genus *Pomacea,* plucked from submerged vegetation in shallow water. This diet was fine when Florida was a wilderness of marshes and meandering rivers, but human development has severely damaged the snail's habitat, and landed the kite on the U.S. Endangered Species List.

Specialists often end up in trouble. The ivory-billed woodpecker specialized in feeding on the grubs of wood-boring beetles, which lived only in old-growth bottomland forests in the South and Mississippi valley. When those forests were cut the ivory-billed couldn't adapt to new environments, and died out in North America. Only a few pairs remain in Cuba.

The willow ptarmigan is found in the arctic of North America, Asia, and Europe. It does not migrate, living through the bleakest conditions imaginable. One reason may be its winter diet of willow buds, which ferment in the intestine to produce alcohol.

The secretary bird of the African plains, so named for the head plumes

The pileated woodpecker feeds mostly on carpenter ants and other insects, but will also eat acorns, seeds, and some fruits and can live in second-growth forests. On the other hand, its nearly extinct relative, the ivory-billed woodpecker, specialized on beetle larva found in old-growth timber, and died out when the forests were cut.

that look like feather pens, is a snake specialist. This raptor is built more like a crane than a hawk, with extremely long legs and short toes. When it finds a snake—even a venomous species—it confuses the reptile with zig-zagging runs and flashes of its open wings, looking for an opening to pin the snake to the ground with its feet. The secretary bird then bludgeons the serpent to death with its wings. Should the snake strike, the bird deflects the bite with its flight feathers, where the teeth or venom can do no harm. In addition to snakes, secretary birds also take lizards, small birds and eggs, rodents, and locusts.

Flower nectar, as any bee knows instinctively, is an excellent source of sugar. So it is not surprising that birds have learned the same thing, and that a few families have come to specialize in the sweet liquid.

The best known are the hummingbirds; more than 300 species feed largely on flower nectar and the tiny insects they find near the tubular blossoms they prefer. Hummers have long bills that sheathe even longer tongues for drinking, while the Old World honeyeaters have tongues that end in a four-pronged, fringed tip. Lories, the small parrots of Australia and surrounding regions, have blunt, fringed tongues perfect for feeding on the open, cuplike flowers native to their homelands.

Tool-using Birds

For years, one of the only recognized instances of a tool-using animal was a species of Galapagos finch. While many other tool users have since come to light, the finch is still a fascinating example of behavioral evolution.

There are fourteen species of Darwin finches, all descended from a single ancestor variety. Some have evolved thick beaks for cracking seeds; others have thinner bills for eating insects. The woodpecker-finch has a stout, curving beak for chopping at wood to expose the bugs beneath. Lacking the woodpecker's long, barbed tongue, the finch snaps off a cactus spine, and uses it to spear the hiding insects.

Another Darwin finch on Wenman Island in the Galapagos chain has turned to vampirism for part of its living, biting the wings of boobies and other seabirds and drinking the blood that flows from the wounds.

Lilliputian Hazards

Hummingbirds, because of their tiny size, fit into the food chain in some very unlikely ways. Occasionally a small, agile raptor such as a sharp-shinned hawk or a merlin will manage to catch a flying hummingbird, and house cats sometimes swat one from the flowerbed, but what other bird must be careful of spiders? A number of North American species have been found entangled in cobwebs, including those of the large yellow-and-black garden spider. Other hummingbirds have fallen victim to praying mantids, frogs, and predatory fish, all of which probably mistook the birds for big insects.

Hummingbirds aren't even safe from other songbirds. There are records of brown-crested flycatchers catching hummingbirds in the Southwest, and orioles have also been known to kill them on rare occasion.

Plant-Bird Interactions

The interactions between birds and the plants on which they feed can be complex and fascinating. A large number of tropical plants have adapted to hummingbirds, providing nectar in return for the unwitting pollination that hummers provide; such "hummingbird plants" are generally red, have abundant nectar (but no scent to attract insects) and bear tubular flowers.

The tropical tree *Erythrina fusca* has a strange adaptation to the orchard oriole, a species that breeds in the eastern United States and winters in Central and South America, where males are fiercely territorial. As the male oriole feeds on the nectar of the tree's flowers it must peel away an outer petal, exposing inner petals with burnt orange color that match the bird's plumage. After the oriole has fed for a time in one tree (and has been covered in the tree's pollen), it is literally scared off by all the burnt orange it sees around it. And so it carries the first tree's pollen off to another *Erythrina* tree, insuring pollination.

The Tennessee warbler is another neotropical migrant that is manipulated by its food plant. An insect eater on its Canadian nesting grounds, it feeds on tree nectar in the tropics during the winter. One tree, the *Combretum,* has bright red pollen that its upright anthers smear across the warbler's face, effectively "war-painting" it as it feeds. Painted warblers are more successful in driving others away from a feeding territory, so the tree helps the warbler secure a food supply, at the same time making it more likely that its own pollen will be carried to another tree.

Chummy Eagles

When food is plentiful, even the most territorial of birds may relax their natural animosity and tolerate others of the same species close by. That explains why several thousand bald eagles gather in relative peace each winter along Alaska's Chilkat River for a salmon run. Birders and other tourists marvel at the sight of trees holding 50 or 100 eagles, and although squabbles do break out over salmon carcasses, on the whole tranquility reigns.

Eelgrass and Geese

The Atlantic race of the brant is a small, dark goose, not much larger than a mallard, that winters on saltwater along the Eastern seaboard. The brant's major food was traditionally an aquatic plant called eelgrass, but in the 1930s an epidemic all but wiped out the eelgrass in the mid-Atlantic region. The brant flocks, deprived of their food, were devastated, but over the years they adapted to a more diverse diet of other aquatic plants, and today brant numbers are climbing. Eelgrass, too, is reappearing, so the future seems brighter for this unusual goose.

Small finches, like these goldfinches at a tube feeder, use a back-and-forth motion of their beaks to crack seeds open, unlike the brute force exerted by larger birds.

Up and Down, Side to Side

Seed-eating birds use two very different methods of cracking open a shell. One group, primarily finches, takes the seed in the beak and slices it open with a back-and-forth action of the lower mandible. The other group, including sparrows, grosbeaks, and cardinals, simply use brute force, cracking the seed with viselike pressure.

Food and Lifestyle

Each bird species has its own unique approach to life, so that even among closely related types there are differences. The hairy woodpecker, a common temperate-forest species, and the three-toed woodpecker of the boreal forest both use their heavy bills and barbed tongues to remove insects from standing timber. But where the hairy woodpecker gets 45 percent of its food by drilling into the bark, 30 percent from gleaning the trunk of the tree, and 25 percent elsewhere, the three-toed obtains 85 percent from drilling, 10 from gleaning, and just 5 percent elsewhere. Flickers, which share much of the same range as the hairy woodpecker, get most of their food on the ground, picking up the ants they love to eat.

Food supply plays a big—often overriding—role in determining when a bird breeds. For most temperate species the time is spring or summer, but for a Mediterranean falcon the biggest bounty comes in autumn.

Eleonora's falcon, a dark, peregrine-sized raptor, breeds on remote cliffsides of the Greek islands. It times its nesting to late summer and early fall, when the songbirds of Europe are starting their southward flight to Africa, and captures those that drop, exhausted, toward the islands. For some reason the falcon hunts almost exclusively over open water, and will not chase those birds that make it to land. Eleonora's falcon is named, incidentally, after a princess of fourteenth-century Sardinia who decreed that nesting raptors be protected.

Each of the world's major rain forest

Harris' Hawks

Harris' hawks are desert dwellers of the Southwest, large soaring hawks with a very unusual lifestyle. They hunt cooperatively in packs, like wolves or African hunting dogs, a trait almost unheard of among raptors.

The key seems to be the hawk's extended family; even during the nesting season, younger birds will help the breeding pair to raise a new batch of chicks. The group also hunts in unison. As many as six Harris' hawks, all related, will patrol their territory together. They take mostly jackrabbits and cottontails, using three tactics: the flush-and-ambush, the surprise pounce, and the relay.

In the flush-and-ambush, the hawks will surround cover where a rabbit is hiding. While the others wait, one hawk goes into the brush, often on foot, to scare the rabbit into the open where the other birds can catch it. In the surprise pounce, the hawks simply converge on a rabbit caught in the open, overpowering it with their superior numbers. And in the relay—especially useful with large, long-distance runners like jackrabbits—the hawks take turns chasing the hare, finally running it to exhaustion and killing it.

In each case, hunting together allows birds that weigh only 2 pounds to kill mammals more than twice that weight. It is the same technique that allows wolves, each weighing about 100 pounds, to kill a moose that weighs 1200 pounds.

Most hawks jealously guard their kills, and even mated pairs may fight with each other for a dead animal. Not so with the Harris' hawk. Once the kill is made, the hawks share the bounty, with the younger birds getting the first chance to eat, instead of the older, more dominant adults.

zones has its own species of giant eagle. In the Philippines and Southeast Asia it is the monkey-eating eagle, a magnificent bird with a heavy, hatchet beak and powerful claws. In the Amazon it is the harpy eagle, and in Africa, the crowned hawk-eagle. All three birds have wide wings and ragged crests, and feed on monkeys, sloths, and other canopy mammals.

A Little Help

Just as a human hunter may use a dog to flush a rabbit, so do some birds use unwitting mammals in their quest for a full stomach. The cattle egret, an African species now naturally established in North America, evolved in association with large grazing animals like Cape buffalo and elephants. In the

FOODS FOR THE FINICKY FEATHERED

Wondering what to offer the avian epicures at your bird feeder? The U.S. Fish and Wildlife Service, which spent two years analyzing food preferences for nearly 20 species of wild songbirds, has the answer.

According to the USFW study, the most widely accepted foods were black, or oil, sunflower seed, a newer variety than the standard striped seed long available; and white proso millet, the choice of such birds as mourning doves, sparrows, and juncos. Here, species by species, is a summary of the results, listing the most popular foods:

American goldfinch: oil sunflower, hulled sunflower, and "thistle" (niger) seed

Blue jay: whole peanut kernels and striped sunflower seed

Brown-headed cowbird: white proso millet

Northern cardinal: oil sunflower

Carolina chickadee: oil sunflower

Dark-eyed junco: red and white proso millet

Common grackle: hulled sunflower and cracked corn

Evening grosbeak: oil sunflower

House finch: oil sunflower and hulled sunflower

House sparrow: German and white proso millet

Mourning dove: oil sunflower and white proso millet

Purple finch: oil sunflower

Red-bellied woodpecker: black-striped sunflower, cracked corn

Song sparrow: white and red proso millet

Starling: peanut hearts and hulled oats

Tree sparrow: red and white proso millet, finely-cracked corn

Tufted titmouse: peanut kernels; oil, black-striped, and gray-striped sunflower

White-crowned sparrow: oil sunflower and white proso millet

White-throated sparrow: oil sunflower, white proso millet, black-striped sunflower, and peanut kernels

United States the egrets follow cows, horses, and even farm machinery, snatching up the insects, frogs, and small mammals that their passage scares into the open.

Also in Africa, a species of hornbill follows monkey troops through the forest canopy, gaining the same benefit as the egrets on the savannah. Several other Old World birds use monkeys as beaters.

Other birds view mammals as mobile buffets. The best known is the African oxpecker, which carefully gleans the wrinkled hides of large animals like hippos, buffalo, and rhinos for ticks and other parasites that are then eaten. In North America the eastern phoebe, a flycatcher, has been seen perching on the backs of white-tailed deer and feeding on the flies and mosquitoes the larger animals attract.

Hatchling solitary vireos gape blindly toward their parents, hoping for an insect. Vireos feed on bugs throughout their lives but even birds that will later switch to a diet of seeds or fruit start life eating insects, which are higher in protein.

Piracy is not unknown among birds; the bald eagle has long been accused of stealing fish from the smaller, more efficient osprey, and while the eagle may not be guilty as often as common knowledge would suggest, it does occasionally swipe a meal.

Among gulls, piracy seems to be a learned behavior, with only a few individuals figuring out how to make a living off the toil of others. Skuas, however, widely practice what biologists call "kleptoparasitism," chasing gannets, puffins, and other smaller seabirds, sometimes pummeling them in midair until they regurgitate their catch. In the tropics, frigatebirds patrol the shoreline, intercepting inbound boobies and mercilessly hounding them into coughing up their fish.

◆ ◆ ◆

5

NUMBERS

We humans like to view the world as we view our kitchen cupboards—a place for everything, everything in its place, all neatly arranged and numbered. But birds defy our best efforts to quantify them, flying seemingly at random, shifting and flickering across vast distances, hiding in jungles, and disappearing below ground. Still, we try anyway, although the numbers that we come up with are often so big that we cannot grasp them.

There are, by estimate (or educated guess) some 100 billion birds in the world, roughly 20 billion of them in North America—and that figure does not include domestic chickens, arguably the most abundant single species with feathers. Sometimes the numbers are so big that they depress instead of amaze: A passenger pigeon flock seen in Kentucky in 1832 was estimated to contain 2.2 billion pigeons, and covered a swath a mile wide and 240 miles long; yet within 82 years, this most abundant of North American birds was extinct.

♦   ♦   ♦

Starlings, Starlings Everywhere

The most common wild bird is probably the European starling, which has been introduced to North America, Africa, Australia, Asia, and many Pacific islands from its native Eurasian range. The house sparrow, similarly carted all over the globe, is a close runner-up; its North American population alone was once estimated at 150 million.

The Wilson's storm-petrel, which breeds along the rim of Antarctica, numbers in the hundreds of millions, and is considered by some to be the second or third most common wild bird. At the other end of the world, the dovekie, a robin-sized auk, breeds in comparable numbers along arctic shorelines.

Zillions of Quelea

In parts of southern Africa, there is a winged scourge that farmers fear. It is not the locust but the quelea, a bird. The red-billed quelea is a pretty weaver-finch, a member of the same group to which the house sparrow belongs. The problem, from an agricultural perspective, is the quelea's numbers—a breeding colony may contain tens of millions of birds, nesting in every tree and shrub over hundreds of acres, and fanning out each day to denude the landscape of food, especially seeds and grain. Because quelea eat grain at a rate of 60 tons per million birds each day, they can have a profound impact on farmers.

Men have struck back with fury. In the 1950s, 100 million quelea migrated with the rains into South Africa, where more than 75 percent were killed with guns, poison, flamethrowers, and explosives. That same year, 6 million adults and 72 million nestlings were killed in what was then Tanganyika. Pressure of that sort would wipe out most birds, but the quelea, with its high reproductive rate, bounced back immediately.

The quelea breeds in response to heavy rains. The breeding cycle is precisely synchronized throughout the colony, so that all the birds are courting, building, and laying at the same time. Hatching is also synchronized; one ob-

server described broken eggshells falling as thick as snow. The quelea colony attracts tremendous numbers of predators, but there are simply too many quelea for the predators to have any real effect. And because the quelea flocks are so nomadic, the predators can't build up in numbers from year to year—a strategy followed by the similarly erratic passenger pigeon.

Back From the Brink

With so many species hovering at the edge of extinction, it is hard to identify the *least* common bird; this dubious honor keeps shifting as one species after another winks out. It's hard not to argue that the honor for the most impressive comeback is held by the Laysan duck, one of several endemic species on this most remote of the Hawaiian islands. The introduction of European rabbits to Laysan in the nineteenth century wiped out the island's vegetation, and imported rats devastated the ground-nesting birds. The one-two punch all but knocked out the Laysan duck, descended from wayward mallards. The rabbits were eliminated by 1923, but the ducks were at the verge of extinction, and a thorough survey of the tiny island in 1930 turned up a single female.

Fortunately for the Laysan duck as a species, that female had mated with the last male before he passed on, and she produced a clutch of fertile eggs. By 1957 the population was up to 600, but the road has been rocky since, dropping again to a few dozen, possibly because of inbreeding.

◆   ◆   ◆

Passenger Pigeons

The passenger pigeon was the most common bird in North America by a country mile—indeed, as mentioned earlier in this chapter, pigeon flocks were often measured in the hundreds of miles. Audubon spent three days watching a pigeon flock fly past, and guessed the birds were passing at a rate of 300 million *an hour.*

The passenger pigeon was a bird of the great eastern and central forests of the United States. Predominantly hardwoods, these forests produced immeasurable quantities of mast—nuts, fruit, and berries—on which the pigeons relied for food, while the massive limbs of these mature trees supported their nesting colonies. About half again as big as the still-common mourning dove and quite similar in appearance, the passenger pigeon differed drastically in its lifestyle. Where the mourning dove is a solitary nester and forms flocks of several hundred at most, the passenger pigeon was genetically programmed to do everything in monstrous groups. Breeding colonies might blanket an area 40 miles square, the trees so heavily laden that the branches broke beneath the weight. At the time North America was settled, the passenger pigeon was unquestionably its most common bird, making up as much as 40 percent of the total avifauna, and may have been the most common bird in the world.

Hungry colonists were quick to capitalize on what seemed to them, for good reason, an inexhaustible supply of food. Millions of the birds were killed by shooting into flocks, but the greatest damage was inflicted on the breeding grounds, where shooting, netting, and poisoning (by sulfur-laden bonfires) were common practices. Trees were cut to get squabs. The pigeons were shipped to market or used for livestock food, a practice that accelerated as rail lines were built.

The pigeon flocks faltered in the East first, but tremendous numbers could still be found in the upper Midwest, so why worry? But the species was in danger on more than one front. The direct assault was bad enough; disturbance in the breeding colonies was often so bad that the pigeons fled the area entirely, and an entire generation would be lost. And the pigeons had only one brood a year, of only a single chick per pair.

Even worse, the forests on which the passenger pigeon relied were being felled at an astounding rate as the demand of lumber increased. This removed both the pigeons' nesting and roosting habitat, as well as its major food supply, since the beech and oak trees that sprouted after timbering would take decades to reach nut-bearing age. Worst of all may have been the development of the telegraph. In earlier years, finding the breeding grounds was a hit-or-miss proposition, since the passenger pigeon was an unpredictable wanderer. But with the telegraph, the travels of the

(Box continues on next page)

72

All that remains of the passenger pigeon multitudes are a few sad, stuffed skins in museums, and paintings like this one by Audubon.

flocks could be precisely traced, and word of their whereabouts sent out once they alighted to nest.

By the 1850s the species had dwindled in the Northeast, and twenty years later it was in serious jeopardy in the Great Lakes region, its last stronghold. Protective laws were passed and promptly ignored; in 1874 at a nesting colony in Michigan, pigeons were killed at a rate of 25,000 a day for nearly a month. The end came quickly, for the passenger pigeon apparently needed the stimulation of great numbers in order to breed. The last wild pigeon was shot in either Wisconsin in 1899 or Ohio in 1900, depending on which account you believe. Captive flocks lived and even bred for a few more years, but the last bird—a female named after Martha Washington—died in the Cincinnati Zoo in 1914.

Dubbed "the white starling" for its explosive population growth, the cattle egret has spread over most of North America since its appearance in Florida in the 1950s. Although quite at home in marshes like most wading birds, cattle egrets also forage in open fields and pastures.

The "White Starling"

The cattle egret has been called the "white starling" because of its explosive debut around the world. In the course of little more than a century, this wading bird has found its way to every continent except Antarctica.

From West Africa, the cattle egret apparently jumped the Atlantic with the help of easterly gales, appearing in Surinam on the South American coast in the 1880s. It spread outward with explosive speed, doing best wherever it found open grassland with nearby marshes, and plenty of large grazing animals. Back in Africa it would follow at the heels of wild grazers, but in the New World, cattle were a fine substitute, chasing up insects and small vertebrates as they grazed.

The cattle egret hit the United States in 1941 at Clewiston, Florida, and within twenty years was found over most of the Southeast and mid-Atlantic region, with colonies as far afield as California. Today it is still spreading rapidly northward, forming huge breeding colonies; stray birds have been reported as far north as the Alaskan panhandle.

Baccalieu's Hidden Birds

At first look, the rugged cliffs, open moors, and scrubby forests of Baccalieu Island off eastern Newfoundland appear to be almost devoid of life. But appearances can be deceiving, because Baccalieu is the site of the largest known bird colony in North America, and one of the biggest in the world.

In most places, a colony of a few thousand birds—even a few hundred—would be considered big. But on Baccalieu, an astonishing 3.3 million Leach's storm-petrels breed. What's more, a visitor in daylight probably wouldn't see a single one.

Storm-petrels are small, gray seabirds, little bigger than swallows, that spend most of their lives at sea, dipping along the surface of the water picking up fish, crustaceans, and plankton. They must come to land to breed, of course, and do so in great colonies on the islands along the Pacific and north Atlantic coasts. The male storm-petrel digs a burrow (up to 6 feet deep in the rocky soil), that ends in a nest chamber where a single egg is laid. Storm-petrels prefer to nest in open, grassy fields, but will burrow in other terrains, even beneath spruce forests.

A staggering number of birds will nest in a small area, all hidden from sight. Storm-petrels come and go only on dark, moonless nights when they are shielded from predators—nights so dark that their vision is useless in finding their nest burrows. Instead, a storm-petrel finds its way home by smell, picking out the particular aroma of its own burrow from the general stench of the colony.

How Many Are There?

Taxonomists fight like cats over which birds belong in what groups, and which are species and which merely subspecies or geographic races, but in round numbers, there are approximately 27 orders of birds worldwide, containing about 155 families and somewhere be-

The yellow-headed blackbird is one of more than 800 bird species found in North America.

The American redstart, shown here in an Audubon painting, is one of many neotropical migrants that are declining sharply in numbers, probably as a result of the rampant destruction of the rain forests, as well as changes in their North American breeding grounds.

tween 8,500 and 9,000 species. The exact number is fluid, since new birds are still being discovered, especially in the cloud-forest valleys of the Andes, where geographic isolation has produced a riot of different species.

Another "Silent Spring"?

When Rachel Carson wrote her classic *Silent Spring* in the early 1960s, she was warning about the misuse of pesticides. Today biologists fear that a silent spring is looming for the forest birds of the East—not from chemicals, but from tropical deforestation and habitat loss on their breeding grounds. The numbers are frightening. Some biologists put the decline of eastern forest songbirds—warblers, vireos, and thrushes in particular—at 50 or even 70 percent. Where once the May woods were filled with waves of migrating birds, today there are only trickles.

The trouble is at least two-fold. As tropical forests are cut and burned, migrants from North America, as well as native Central and South American species, lose their homes. Many species of forest birds that breed over wide areas of North America winter in relatively small areas in the tropics, so that destruction in a single region may doom them; by some estimates, the loss of an acre of rain forest is equal to 8 acres of temperate forest.

It was once thought that migrants were the "new kids on the block" in the tropical forests, existing around the edges of native birds' territories, or on marginal habitat. Were that the case, clearing the forest might not be so harmful for them, since they could be expected to adapt to the changing circumstances. Recent studies, however, have shown that migrants are as finely tuned to their tropical homes as they are to the northern forests, with specific niches (see Chapter 4 for more information on feeding adaptations). While a few neotropical migrants may weather the storm of changes, most will fare poorly. The problem isn't only in Central and South America. Birds like the red-eyed vireo, which winters in the largely untouched Amazon Basin, are also declining, suggesting that there is trouble up north, too. Its name is fragmentation.

Most of the neotropical migrants nest in large, unbroken tracts of forest, and they do poorly when the woods are cut into smaller and smaller pieces. Each isolated woodlot functionally becomes an island (in fact, the study of such situations is known as island biogeography), leaving the birds cut off from each other and from crucial habitats. Perhaps worst of all, fragmentation opens up the forest to outside dangers—predators like blue jays and grackles that prefer edge habitat rather than deep woods; and the brown-headed cowbird, which parasitizes the nests of other songbirds. Because the cowbird is a recent addition to eastern birdlife, having expanded into the region in the early 1900s, many neotropical migrants have no instinctive defenses, like the ability to recognize a cowbird egg and eject it; further, their nests tend to be open cups, easily found by female cowbirds.

Scientists are finding that the effects of a road, field, or housing development extend beyond the edge of the trees, and reach far back into the

For reasons that are not clear, the northern mockingbird—along with the cardinal and a few other species—has been expanding its range northward at a remarkable rate.

woods. A forest of 1,000 acres with five 10-acre clearcuts loses more than 5 percent of its woods; because of this edge effect, a much larger percentage of the forest will be rendered unsuitable for some forest-dwelling songbirds.

On the Upswing

Not all wild birds are declining. According to a long-running survey of the continent's birdlife, a number of species are expanding their numbers and ranges at remarkable rates.

The data comes from the Breeding Bird Survey, conducted each spring since 1965 by the U.S. Fish and Wildlife Service and the Canadian Wildlife Service. Observers travel 25-mile routes, stopping every half-mile for three minutes to watch and listen for, and record birds. Because the same routes are run year after year, the BBS provides an excellent way to monitor population trends.

Perhaps no other songbird has grown in numbers and range more than the house finch, illegally imported from the American West to New York in the 1940s, and released. So far out of range and habitat, the red-breasted imports should have perished. Instead, like starlings and house sparrows before them, they took over like an invading army, increasing by as much as 20 percent a year. House finches now occupy most of the United States east of the Mississippi, and are advancing West, where they will presumably meet with their stay-at-home cousins in a few years.

Other songbirds that are expanding their range include northern mockingbirds, spreading from their magnolia-belt home as far north as Ontario; the American robin (heading south) and the northern cardinal (heading north), both apparently in response to housing developments that provide ideal habitat; evening grosbeaks moving east, perhaps in response to more and more winter bird feeders; and golden-crowned kinglets, moving south from one Norway spruce plantation to the next. A change from round highway culverts to square models have given cave and cliff swallows new nesting areas (they like the corners), and they have responded by moving into fresh areas of the South.

Extinct North American Birds

S ince 1600, five species and two subspecies of mainland North American birds have become extinct, and several others are so rare that they may well be gone completely.

The first casualty was the great auk, a flightless puffin relative found in the North Atlantic from Scotland to Newfoundland, and the original "pen gwyn," as Welsh sailors dubbed it. (The name was later extended to include unrelated penguins of the Southern Hemisphere.) Big, meaty, and common on many offshore islands, they were a target for egg collectors and favored fare for sailors and whalers, who massacred them by the thousands. The last was killed off Iceland in 1844, with a final sighting near Newfoundland in 1852.

If the demise of the great auk was no mystery, the extinction of the Labrador duck is. Also known as the pied duck, it was never common, even on its main winter home off Long Island, and (presumably) at its nesting ground somewhere on the foggy coast of northeastern Canada. Because the Labrador duck fed heavily on mussels and tasted strongly of shellfish, it was never hunted to the same degree as other waterfowl. Nevertheless, by the 1850s it was noticeably rare, and the last bird was shot

Hunted for its oil and meat, the great auk—the largest of the auks, and completely flightless—was driven to extinction just a few years after Audubon painted it in 1834.

(Box continues on next page)

The Labrador duck is an extinction enigma. Apparently never common, it disappeared from the Northeast coast before scientists could even find its breeding grounds. Audubon, who looked for it unsuccessfully in the Canadian Maritimes, painted this pair from specimens sent him by a hunter in Massachusetts.

in 1878. Experts now speculate that the Labrador duck may have nested on only a few islands, where egg collecting may have pushed it over the edge.

The Bachman's warbler is, like the Labrador duck, an enigma. Discovered in 1832 by Audubon's close friend the Reverend John Bachman, it dropped out of sight until the 1890s, after which it was considered fairly common in parts of the South. By the 1920s it was vanishing again; the last nest was found in 1938, and the last bird on breeding territory in 1963. The felling of southern forests certainly played a role, as perhaps did the destruction of bamboo canebrakes on which the bird may have relied. It has not been seen in the United States for several years, and the most recent sighting was of a single bird in 1981 in Cuba. Bachman's warbler is extinct, or a hair's-breadth from it.

Also unsure is the status of the Eskimo curlew, a shorebird with a gracefully curving beak that was shot for meat in the 1800s. Once one of the most common shorebirds, the "doughbird" has been declared extinct

(Box continues on next page)

a number of times in the past half-century, but keeps confounding those who would write it off. Last reported in 1925, it shocked ornithologists when a single bird was seen in Texas in 1962. Since then, Eskimo curlews have been reported every few years along the Texas coast, and a few have been found breeding in the arctic. Like the Bachman's warbler, the curlew could wink out without our ever knowing it.

The destruction of hardwood swamps in the South and the Mississippi Valley doomed the ivory-billed woodpecker, a magnificent, crow-sized bird with a flaming red crest and white beak. Entirely dependent on mature stands of trees where wood-boring beetle larvae were common, the ivory-billed couldn't adapt to the frenzy of logging that swept the region in the past 150 years. By the 1960s it had dwindled to just a half-dozen birds, and there have been no reliable reports in years. A tiny population of Cuban ivory-bills was discovered in 1986, but they, too, are beset by heavy logging, and their future is bleak.

The extinction of the passenger pigeon in 1914 frequently overshadows the loss, four years later, of an equally remarkable bird, the Carolina parakeet. A vibrant beauty of orange, green, and yellow, it was the only native parrot in the East, and was especially common in the South. It was also an agricultural pest of some proportion, descending in great flocks on or-

The trumpeter swan is a conservation success story. By the 1930s the population in the contiguous states of America had been reduced to a handful of birds in a remote Montana valley, but today its numbers are growing, and it has been reintroduced to parts of its former range.

(Box continues on next page)

chards and fields. Millions were shot for crop protection, as well as for the feather trade; others were captured for cage birds.

The heath hen was the eastern subspecies of the greater prairie chicken, adapted to brushy forest openings along the Atlantic coast. Abundant and easy to kill, it no doubt figured in the first Thanksgiving, and in many subsequent colonial meals (at one point, servants in Boston petitioned that they not be forced to eat heath hen more than twice a week). It disappeared from most of New England by 1840, from Long Island by 1844, and from the blueberry barrens of Pennsylvania's Pocono plateau by 1870.

A tiny group lingered into the twentieth century on Martha's Vineyard off the Massachusetts coast, however. By 1916 there were more than 2,000 and if anyone had thought to move some of them to new locations (a common practice today with endangered species) we might still have heath hens. But no one did, and a wildfire on the island that year reduced the population to 150. Poachers and a thriving colony of feral housecats finished the job, despite special wardens. By 1928 there was just one male, doing his mating dance to a tragically empty world. He died three years later.

Another subspecies to disappear—this time in the Space Age—was the dusky seaside sparrow. Once common in the St. John's salt marshes of eastern Florida, this subspecies of the widespread seaside sparrow suffered from development (including the nearby Cape Canaveral space complex), ditching of marshes, and spraying for mosquitoes. By 1980 only five males were left, which were crossbred with closely related Scott's seaside sparrows in an attempt to preserve at least some of their genetic heritage. The last pure male died in 1987, and the only four crossbreeds died or escaped in 1989 when a storm smashed their enclosure at Walt Disney World. As a final indignity, genetic research on tissue from the last duskies suggests they were not even a full subspecies after all, but a mere color form of the widespread seaside sparrows.

Fooling Mother Nature to Help Mother Nature

In the battle to save endangered species, ingenuity is the name of the game. Biologists must be creative to overcome the many problems facing rare birds:

• To attract rare dark-rumped petrels to specially built, predator-proof nest burrows in the Galapagos Islands,

The whooping crane is one endangered bird that benefits from a ruse known as "double-clutching," in which the first clutch of eggs are removed from the nest and placed in an incubator, spurring the adults to remate and lay a second batch.

THREATENED AND ENDANGERED U.S. BIRDS

The following species and subspecies are listed as threatened or endangered under the U.S. Endangered Species Act (when this book went to press). Subspecies are marked with an asterisk.

ENDANGERED MAINLAND BIRDS

Masked bobwhite quail*
California condor
Mississippi sandhill crane*
Whooping crane
Eskimo curlew
Bald eagle (except where listed as threatened)
American peregrine falcon*
Northern aplomado falcon*
Aleutian Canada goose*
Everglades snail kite
Puerto Rican nightjar
Puerto Rican parrot

Brown pelican (Louisiana, Texas, California)
Puerto Rican plain pigeon
Piping plover (Great Lakes watershed)
Attwater's greater prairie chicken*
California clapper rail*
Light-footed clapper rail*
Yuma clapper rail*
San Clemente loggerhead shrike*
Cape Sable seaside sparrow*
Dusky seaside sparrow (extinct)*

Florida grasshopper sparrow*
Wood stork
California least tern*
Least tern (inland populations)
Roseate tern (Atlantic coast south to North Carolina)
Black-capped vireo
Least Bell's vireo*
Bachman's warbler
Kirtland's warbler
Ivory-billed woodpecker
Red-cockaded woodpecker

THREATENED MAINLAND BIRDS

Audubon's crested caracara*
Bald eagle (Washington, Oregon, Minnesota, Wisconsin, Michigan)

Arctic peregrine falcon*
Florida scrub jay*
Piping plover (except where listed as endangered)

San Clemente sage sparrow*
Roseate tern (in Florida, Puerto Rico and Virgin Islands)
Inyo brown towhee*

ENDANGERED HAWAIIAN BIRDS

Hawaii akepa
Maui akepa
Kauai akialoa
Akiapolaau
Hawaiian coot
Hawaii creeper
Molokai creeper
Oahu creeper
Hawaiian crow
Hawaiian duck
Laysan duck

Laysan finch
Nihoa finch
Hawaiian goose (nene)
Hawaiian hawk
Crested honeycreeper
Nihoa millerbird
Hawaiian moorhen
Nukupu'u
Kauai o'o
'O'u
Palila

Maui parrotbill
Hawaiian dark-rumped petrel
Po'ouli
Newell's Townsend's shearwater (threatened)
Hawaiian stilt
Large Kauai thrush
Molokai thrush
Small Kauai thrush

tape recorders broadcast the sounds of a huge petrel colony, fooling the threatened birds into thinking they had lots of company.

- In Bermuda, the cahow petrel—believed extinct from the mid-1600s to 1916—suffers from competition with aggressive tropicbirds, which steal nest burrows and kill the cahow chicks. But because tropicbirds are fractionally the bigger of the two, wooden entrance baffles exclude them, but permit cahows to enter.

- The Puerto Rican parrot also suffers from nest competition—from the pearly-eyed thrasher. Researchers found that if they provided a smaller nest box for the thrashers near the parrot's big nest cavity, not only would the thrashers stay out of the parrots' way themselves—they would chase away all other thrashers, too.

- Many endangered birds benefit from a biological hiccup called "double-clutching"—that is, if the pair's first attempt at nesting is removed, they will often lay a second (and even third) clutch. This approach has been taken with whooping cranes and California condors, among other birds.

- Transplanting birds from one area to another isn't terribly novel, but when biologists decided to reintroduce puffins to Maine from Newfoundland, they used tape recorded calls and wooden puffin decoys to mimic a big colony, luring the birds back to the release site in subsequent years.

- To prevent captive-hatched California condors from "imprinting" on their keepers—that is, from forming a bond with whatever large creature happens to be feeding them—zoo employees use realistic hand puppets built to resemble adult condor heads. The artificial stand-ins "regurgitate" the meal (in this case diced mice) just as a real condor parent would.

- The introduced brown tree snake has decimated the birdlife of Guam, including the Micronesian kingfisher, white tern, and Guam rail. To reduce the number of snakes on this Pacific island, the Guam Division of Aquatic and Wildlife Resources has distributed recipes for sweet-and-sour snake and snake adobo to the locals. Meanwhile, researchers are trying to synthesize the female snake's sexual pheromone, in the hope that it can be used to bait snake traps.

Guam Rail: You Can't Go Home Again

The Guam rail—one of the victims of the brown tree snake—is a secretive bird that was once so abundant that the island had a legal hunting season. But while the birds could handle hunting pressure, they couldn't stand the constant predation from the snakes, introduced after World War II to combat rats, another human introduction. The rail population went from 80,000 in 1968 to just 100 in 1983.

By 1989, all 138 remaining rails were living in zoos in Guam and the United States. Biologists were ready to reintroduce a few to the wild, but not on Guam—the snakes would simply eat the releasees. Their new home was to

Saving the California Condor

No other endangered species arouses such passions as the California condor, the largest bird in North America—and one of the rarest. Only 29 remain, all in captivity.

The condor was not always so rare, although its fortunes began to wane at the end of the last ice age. Fossils have been found in New York, Florida, and the Southwest, but by the time Europeans appeared on the scene, it was restricted to the Pacific coast from Mexico to British Columbia. Lewis and Clark had a dickens of a time keeping condors away from the elk their hunters shot during the winter the expedition spent at the mouth of the Columbia River, but the bird was so big—and such an inviting target—that it began to decline almost as soon as less responsible whites showed up in the neighborhood.

By the end of the nineteenth century, it was restricted to California and Baja California; four decades later it had made a last stand in a rugged, remote stretch of southern California. The numbers at that point were low—about 60 birds—and getting lower with each passing year. Part of the problem was continued illegal shooting, accidental poisoning from carcasses set out for coyotes, and an overall "dirty" environment polluted with a variety of toxins. Another part of the problem was the condor's own breeding biology; maturity isn't reached until age six, and a pair lays only one egg every other year. It was a recipe for trouble.

The standard approach to saving a threatened species—protection and habitat preservation—simply didn't work with the condor. Despite two large reserves, despite trucking in frozen roadkills (referred to as "condor-sicles"), despite intensive field study, radio telemetry and public education efforts, condors continued to disappear, often with no explanation. The tally in 1978 was a mere 25 birds—and with each new loss, another piece of irreplaceable genetic material was lost forever.

The recovery program took a dramatic turn in the 1980s, with the decision to capture some of the condors and form a captive flock that could eventually be used to restock the wild—an approach that had worked well with whooping cranes. The decision was reached after bitter debate, with many condor advocates claiming it was better to let the species disappear than subject it to the "indignity" of captivity. They were eventually overruled, and eggs were taken from wild nests (spurring the pairs to reclutch), hatched and placed with other captive condors. The plan, to build a captive flock while maintaining wild condors, seemed to be coming along well.

But the winter of 1984–85 was horrific for the condors. Six of the eight remaining wild birds died, leaving just one pair alive. The female was caught in June 1986 (ironically, on the same day that her chick hatched

(Box continues on next page)

86

in the San Diego Wild Animal Park). Her mate—the last free-flying condor—was caught in April 1987, having eluded biologists for nearly a year.

With all 27 condors in captivity, the paramount question was whether the species would reproduce in captivity. Work with the related Andean condor suggested they would, and so it proved. The first condor egg conceived in a zoo hatched in April 1988, and a second hatched a year later. The rate, while slow, should pick up momentum as more of the younger birds reach maturity and begin breeding.

A stickier issue, biologically and politically, is where to release the condors when the captive flock is big enough, perhaps by the mid-1990s. The original California range remains a toxic, dangerous place, and some authorities have argued for the Grand Canyon area, where the condors would have solitude and a clean environment, or even the Northwest coast. Others balk at the idea of removing the condor from California. By early 1990, a group of captive-bred female Andean condors had been released in two sites in southern California, to test reintroduction techniques, and the question of whether the California condor will eventually come home to roost remained undecided.

One of the most critically endangered birds in the world, the California condor now exists only in captivity, although biologists plan to re-introduce it into the wild when the captive population reaches a higher level.

be Rota, another small island in the Marianas chain, where tree snakes are not found. The first six rails were released in December 1989, with another 30 to follow a few months later. The hope is to build a healthy population on Rota, so that if the tree snake can be controlled on Guam, the rails can be reintroduced to their real home.

Dodos Weren't Such Dodos

Sailors considered dodos so stupid that their very name has become synonymous with lack of intelligence, but dodos weren't stupid. Like many island birds, these relatives of the pigeons simply had no experience with predators, and didn't know to flee from the hairy-faced things on two legs.

The dodo may be the most famous extinct bird of all, although the name usually covers three related birds from three Indian Ocean islands: the Mauritius dodo, the solitaire on the island of Rèunion, and the Rodriguez solitaire. All were large (up to 50 pounds), flightless birds with big, hooked beaks, tiny wings, stout legs, and short, curly tail feathers.

Sailors being the ravenous group they are, the dodos and solitaires were viewed as food, although equal damage was inflicted by introduced rats, pigs, and monkeys. The dodo was extinct by 1680, the Rèunion solitaire by 1750, and the Rodriguez solitaire by about 1800.

Rare Eagle

The Madagascar serpent eagle, believed extinct since 1930, when it was last seen, was rediscovered in 1988 in the Marojejy Reserve. The good news may be short-lived; the reserve is under intense pressure from slash-and-burn agriculture, and scientists fear that this unusual, crested eagle may disappear for good as its habitat is cut.

◆　◆　◆

6

FOLKLORE AND LEGENDS

The magpie is a pretty bird—black hood, white belly, boldly marked wings, and a long, iridescent green tail. But in much of Britain, it is considered a bird of bad omen. The reasons are lost in antiquity, but until fairly recently rural folk believed in the old saying "One for sorrow, two for joy"—the notion that seeing a single magpie would bring misfortune, but two, happiness. As with most of these old portents of doom, there was a way out: spit three times over your right shoulder while saying "Devil, devil, I defy thee."

Every culture on Earth has myths, legends, or folklore about birds. In the Mediterranean, the kingfisher, or *halcyon,* was thought to be able to calm the seas during its incubation period. Today, we know such tranquility as the halcyon days—just one example of how bird folklore pervades even modern life.

◆　◆　◆

The Bird-gods of Egypt

The ancient Egyptians might not have been the first civilization to worship birds and incorporate them into their religion, but they certainly pursued the idea with the greatest zeal.

One of the incarnations of Thoth, the god of wisdom and learning, was the sacred ibis, a black-and-white waterbird now quite rare over most of its Middle Eastern range. In statuary and paintings, Thoth is often shown as a man with an ibis's head and curving beak, with the round disk of the sun topping its headdress. Horus, the Sky Lord, was depicted as having the head of a falcon, complete with the notched beak and dark "mustache" facial markings of a real falcon.

To gain the intercession of these gods, the ancient Egyptians sacrificed

The raven was loathed as a symbol of impending death and war to Europeans, while to the Native Americans of the Pacific Northwest, the bird was considered a supernatural trickster and creator.

animals to them—the same animals whose forms the gods were thought to assume. The sacrifices were mummified and stored away in tombs, in numbers that defy belief. In a temple at Saqqara in the sixth century B.C., penitents offered up nearly a million falcons and as many as 8 million ibis, each mummified, wrapped carefully in linen, and stored in clay pots. The numbers of ibis are so great that only some form of intensive, domestic rearing could have supplied the demand, although the falcons, which cannot be raised easily in captivity, must have come from the wild.

Ravens: Cads and Creators

Ravens have been birds of omen and legend for millennia, perhaps because of their size, obvious intelligence, black plumage, and habit of feeding on battlefield corpses.

Probably the best-known raven legend claims that England will not fall while ravens live in the Tower of London. The metropolitan area is hardly good raven habitat, but the government keeps tame, wing-clipped birds on the grounds to satisfy the requirements of the legend.

In the Faroe Islands, between Scotland and Iceland, the raven was believed to possess a "victory stone" with magical properties. When the adult ravens were away from the nest, islanders would steal their eggs, boil them hard and return them unseen, on the theory that the raven would get the stone from a secret place and set it beside the eggs to cure them; the stone then had to be removed from the nest before the eggs

hatched. A victory stone was considered potent magic, bestowing wealth, popularity, and invulnerability from attacks by humans and trolls alike. In Iceland, a raven's stone was thought capable of making the bearer invisible. (In Scotland's Orkney Islands, a crow is said to have flown to the Holy Land for a magical cure for her eggs, boiled as a joke by lead miners. Before she left, however, she caused the cliff over the mine to collapse, killing all the miners except one who had argued against harming the eggs.)

For most people of the Middle Ages, the raven was an ill omen, largely because of its scavenging habits; it was the bird that waited near the gibbet, ready to pluck the eyes from a hanged convict. Soldiers, noting how ravens followed armies and gathered by the hundreds at the scene of battle, had superstitions about this largest of perching birds—a tradition dating back to ancient Greece, and continuing to the present day. How ominous would Poe's lines have been if he had written: "Quoth the bluebird, Nevermore."?

By contrast, the Indians of the Pacific Northwest revered the raven as the creator of the world—but also as a trickster who used his guile sometimes against humans, sometimes for their benefit. According to one legend, the raven created the land after he tired of flying over the empty ocean. Raven dropped pebbles into the water that grew into islands, forming the rich archipelago along the Pacific coast. These he filled with birds and animals, and finally humans, fashioned from wood and clay.

One of the most pervasive Raven myths tells how the great bird stole the sun from the lodge of the Sky Chief, who kept it hidden, leaving the world in darkness. Raven changed himself into a spruce needle floating in a spring. The needle was swallowed by the chief's daughter; she later gave birth to a baby, who was Raven in disguise. The baby convinced Sky Chief to give him the sun as a plaything. With that Raven changed back to his bird form and flew off, taking the sun back to the sky and bringing light to the world.

Omens On the Wing

Death and birds are inexplicably linked in many cultures. In parts of Scotland, the croaking of a corn crake (a species of rail) in a field meant that someone in the neighborhood would die. The same was foreseen if a raven or a crow circled the roof of a house and called, or if a rooster crowed at midnight.

In Europe—and later in America—a bird at the window meant death, as did a crow calling three times while flying over a house. The repetitious night calls of the whip-poor-will were frequently considered an omen of death, but the calls were also important to unmarried women. If the whip-poor-will called once, she would not marry for at least a year. If it called three times or more, she would be a spinster all her life. The magic number was two calls, which meant impending matrimony. She could also wish for marriage the instant she heard the first *whip-poor-will-l-l-l*, but the wish would come true only if she kept it a secret.

◆　◆　◆

Water-walkers

Next to soldiers, there is probably no more superstitious lot on earth than sailors, living as they do at the whim of the unpredictable and often violent ocean. Over the centuries, sailors have built up a host of beliefs about the seabirds that cross their paths and follow their ships.

The storm-petrels, the dove-sized birds so common in the waters of the Southern Hemisphere, have perhaps the greatest store of legend and folklore swirling about them. Even their name comes from the belief that their appearance augurs storms, and indeed, flocks frequently seem to ride the advancing weather fronts. The word "petrel" is thought to be a diminutive of Peter, as in St. Peter, the apostle who walked on water; storm-petrels feed by hovering just at the surface, dabbling the water with their feet as though walking across the liquid. The colloquial name for these birds is "Mother Carey's chickens," apparently a corruption of *Mater Cara,* the Holy Mother, whose protection has been sought by sailors since time immemorial.

The albatross was viewed with suspicion as the harbinger of bad weather, especially gale winds and fog, but to kill one was to invite bad luck—not that this stopped seafarers from killing them on their breeding grounds for meat and, more importantly, for feathers. In the nineteenth century, tens of thousands were slaughtered, reducing one species—the short-tailed albatross—to fewer than 50 birds; about 200 exist today. The albatross's unusual name, incidentally, traces back to the Portuguese word *álcatraz,* a large bird

Dabbling on the stormy surface of the open sea, the Leach's storm-petrel was seen by superstitious sailors as an omen of storms. The way in which it appears to walk on water inspired them to name it after St. Peter, while another common name for the bird referred to the Virgin Mary.

with pointed wings; this later became *algotross,* and finally its current form, although these birds have been known to seamen as goonies (for their tameness around humans) or mollymawks, from a Dutch word meaning "stupid gull."

Weather and Birds

Birds, being creatures of the air, have long been considered omens of the weather—and often with good reason, because meteorological changes obviously have the greatest impact on flying animals. The old saying that low-flying geese mean rain is firmly founded in the principle of barometric pressure.

In the days when every farm had a flock of geese, fall was the traditional butchering season, since the fowl would be a burden to feed over the winter. The color of the breastbone was said to forecast the coming winter— cold if the bone is cloudy, mild if it is pale, but bitter and snowy if it is red. In ancient Rome, a thick wing bone meant a hard winter, a thin one, mild.

The autumn migration was watched with interest, since an early flight of geese meant a hard winter, but flocks going *north* might mean a mild, open season ahead. In the shorter term, songbirds feeding close to the house, or feed-

Birds have long been considered to be weather indicators; the color of a goose's breastbone, for example, was thought to predict the severity of the upcoming winter.

ing with unusual intensity, were taken as a sign of an approaching snow-storm—a good guess because the lowering air pressure ahead of a front usually triggers a feeding frenzy among many kinds of wild animals.

Bird sounds have always been taken as clues to the weather. Geese honk before storms, bobwhite quail were said to call to the approaching rain, and the yellow-billed cuckoo was long known as the "storm crow" because it often calls monotonously before a rain.

Maine lobstermen, in the days before radar-assisted forecasting, relied on the flight of gulls. If the gulls headed out to sea at daybreak, then it was considered safe for men to do so, but if the gulls stayed close to shore, bad weather was coming.

BIRD-RELATED WEATHER FOLKLORE

- If chickens run for shelter when it rains, the shower will be brief. If they stay outside, it will last a long time.
- Low-flying swallows mean rain; high-flying swallows mean fair weather.
- A rooster crowing at dusk foretells rain.
- A large flock of crows is a sign of impending rain.
- When a European skylark flies high and sings loudly, fair weather is at hand.
- Ruffled feathers on a turkey, pigeons staying in the roost, and screaming guinea fowl all mean rain.
- Heavy toe fringes on ruffed grouse mean a bad winter (grouse grow such fringes each winter to keep from sinking in snow).
- Swallows nesting in a barn protects it from lightning.

Owls and the Supernatural

Owls, with their nocturnal habits and spooky calls, are naturals for the role of death-bringers, witches' familiars, and the like. On the isle of Sicily, an owl calling near the home of a sick man is a terrible development, for it means that the man will die in three days; if no one in the home is ill, the call portends a tonsil infection. Among some of the Indian tribes of the Pacific Northwest, an owl will call out the name of a person who is to die, while some of the Woodland tribes of the Northeast thought witches could assume the form of owls, then suck away the life of a sleeping rival.

An owl's tidings are not always bad—at least depending on one's viewpoint. In Wales, the cry of an owl meant the impending loss of virginity, not necessarily unwelcomed news to many young people. In southern France, the scream of a barn owl in the chimney of a pregnant woman means the birth of a girl (bad news for farming folk), but a dash of salt in the fire may change the outcome.

Among French peasants, the scream of a barn owl in the chimney was thought to presage the birth of a girl. Since barn owls often nest in unused flues, the situation was much more common than might be expected.

(Box continues on next page)

Legends, beliefs, and myths about owls seem numberless. In ancient Greece, as in Rome (which adopted many Greek beliefs), the owl was a bird of bad omen, a thought carried through to Shakespeare's day; in *Julius Caesar* the owl is numbered among the portents of doom:

> And yesterday the bird of night did sit
> Even at noon-day upon the market-place
> Hooting and shrieking . . .

In Africa, owls were feared as the hired killers of witch doctors, while the Ainu people of northern Japan capped their homes with wooden owls to break a famine or epidemic. In many parts of Europe and the Mediterranean basin, owl eggs are considered a cure for alcoholism—or a preventive, if given to a child. They were also considered a cure for epilepsy and even gray hair. The owl's heart was thought by Greek magicians to be able to draw the truth from a lying woman, if placed upon her breast (one can only wonder what sorts of things a lady would blurt out if a bloody bird heart were slapped on her chest without warning). Pliny the Elder discounted this as "a monstrous lie," while at the same time recommending burnt owl's foot as a snake repellent. As an indication of the longevity of folk beliefs, consider this: Using an owl's heart to divine the truth was recommended as late as the 1860s among the rural Pennsylvania Germans.

Primitive medicine placed great store in owls. Their eyes, when eaten, prevented blindness and improved vision, especially night sight. (The English believed the same was true of the eggs—certainly more palatable.) Water brushed on an infant's eyes with an owl feather was thought by some American Indians to improve vision and the ability to stay awake at night, while in India, a healthy helping of owl meat was considered an aphrodisiac—but with its use came the risk of madness.

There is a strange dichotomy about beliefs in owls—that they are evil omens on one hand, but symbols of wisdom on the other. The idea of the "wise old owl" probably stems from a combination of physical attributes and ancient history. Owls have large, front-facing eyes, flat faces, and slow, studied movements of the head, all of which are adaptations to nocturnal hunting, but which conspire to make the birds look vaguely human. The Greeks, who worshiped Athene as the goddess of wisdom, first chose the owl as her consort. The rest, as they say, is history.

Old Myths, Real Birds

Where do mythical birds come from? As with many of the animals in ancient bestiaries, from the garbled descriptions of real animals by travelers, and inexplicable body parts brought back from distant lands. The classic example is the tusk of the narwhal, which was thought to come from the unicorn.

On the second of his seven legendary voyages, Sinbad the Sailor was reputed to have been shipwrecked on an island occupied by the roc, a bird of monumental proportions. To escape the island, Sinbad roped himself to the sleeping bird, which unwittingly carried him to the mainland the next day. The medieval Arabs were great sailors, with trade routes that stretched east to China and south along the coast of Africa. The African route would have taken them past the island of Madagascar, home to the 10-foot-tall, flightless elephant bird, now thought to be the germ of truth behind the mythical roc.

A legend widespread among Native American tribes was that of the thunderbird, a huge bird that carried the rain on its back and made the lightning and thunder. Thunderbird legends are especially prevalent in the West, leading some to believe that the California condor was the root of the story. But in precontact days the condor was fairly common from California to British Columbia, and wouldn't have been especially mysterious to the Indians.

So what was the thunderbird? One intriguing theory holds that the thunderbird legend is a memory of a much larger vulture, *Teratornis merriami,* that died out following the ice age, but which, for a time, shared North

Owls, like this great horned owl, have inspired reverence and awe in humans who see them as a link to the supernatural.

America with Paleolithic hunters. Twice as heavy as a California condor, it may have been the largest bird to ever fly. If any bird deserved to be memorialized in legend, *Teratornis* was it.

One mythical bird with no known roots in the real world is the phoenix, belief in which arose around 500 B.C. in the Middle East, and was later carried to Europe by returning Crusaders. The phoenix was male, and lived for 500 years. At the end of its life, it built a pyre of sticks and frankincense on which it settled, facing the sun, then erupted into flames. From the ashes arose a new phoenix, which eventually carried the ashes of its predecessor to the altar of the sun.

Native American Creation Stories

Like the Raven stories of the Pacific Northwest tribes, the creation myths of many Native American cultures involved birds, though not always as the creator itself.

Among the Lenni Lenape of New Jersey and Pennsylvania, birds were instrumental in saving the mother of all people, and making dry land. According to the tale, the chief of the Sky People dreamt that he would die if he did not uproot the Tree of Light that grew in the Sky Country, so he and his brothers felled the tree, ripping a hole in the fabric of the sky and revealing the watery world below. Through this hole the Sky Chief threw his pregnant wife, telling her to populate the new world. As she

In one version of the Lenni Lenape creation story, a loon brought a speck of mud to the surface of the lake that once covered the world, thus helping to make the first dry land.

fell, thousands of birds rose through the sky and caught her on their backs, gently depositing her on the back of the mud turtle.

There was no dry land, so the waterbirds and animals dove far below the surface, looking for mud. In some accounts, the turtle fetches the mud itself; in others, it is a muskrat that drowns in the attempt, but floats back to the top with a speck of mud between its toes. Still other accounts give credit to the loon, known as the best diver of the northern lakes. The woman places the soil on the turtle's back and blows on it and it expands to become the world, supported to this day by the patient turtle.

A variation on this theme is found among the Crow of the northern Plains, whose creator was a trickster figure similar to Raven, known as Old Man Coyote. One Crow legend has Old Man Coyote swimming across the watery Earth, bored that he is alone and has no dry land to walk on. He meets two ducks "with red eyes" (possibly grebes), one of which dives far underwater and comes up with a lump of mud, over which Old Man blows to form the earth.

Still using mud, Old Man Coyote makes people and animals (and after a reminder from all the lonely males, he also makes females of each). But when the animals are bored with eating and mating, Old Man Coyote makes a special bird, using bear claws for wings, caterpillar hair for feet, leaves for a tail, and buffalo sinew for a beak. The odd result puzzles all the other animals, but Old Man Coyote tells the bird (a prairie chicken) that although it isn't pretty, it possesses a special power. And so dance is born, in the shuffling mating ritual of the prairie chicken.

Unlike the omnipotent deities of Western culture, the trickster-creators of the Plains Indians were as apt to be the butt of jokes and mishaps as to be their perpetrator. So it was with Na'pi, the Old Man of the Blackfoot. In a legend recorded by Audubon Society founder George Bird Grinnell in the late 1800s, Old Man is walking through the woods one day when he sees a small bird that can make its eyes pop out of its head and fasten onto a tree. Old Man is so taken with this trick that he asks the bird to teach it to him. The bird does so, but warns Old Man that he can only do the trick three times a day.

Predictably, Old Man disregards the advice and makes his eyes pop a fourth time, then can't call them back. He wanders the woods, blind and starving, until a wolf begins to taunt him with a piece of buffalo meat that Old Man can smell but not find. In anger, he snatches out one of the wolf's eyes and sticks them in his own head, so that at last he is able to find his own eyes.

Old Beliefs

It would be easy to laugh at past generations for ludicrous beliefs and oddball notions about birds, if science were not constantly proving equally bizarre ideas to be true—for instance, that screech-owls snatch insect-eating snakes for nest sanitation (more about that in Chapter 8).

Still, many old bits of bird folklore once taken as fact have been shown to be false, like the idea that sparrows spontaneously generated from horse-hair and mud, or the persistent idea, in vogue until the 1700s, that birds hibernate *en masse* at the bottom of the ocean and lakes. That one started (as did so much other natural history nonsense) with the Greeks, who were actually making a reasoned hypothesis based on available information. They knew the birds flew south each fall, disappearing over the Mediterranean, and returned from the sea each spring. They also knew from first-hand observation that turtles and frogs hibernate in mud, and that swallows gathered in great numbers along the shores of lakes. Given their understanding of the situation, the concept of hibernating birds was perfectly logical (and not totally wrong, as the discovery of that hibernating poorwill in Arizona proved).

The goose barnacle gets its name from the long, rubbery stalk that attaches this crustacean to ships, whales, or pilings. To the ancients, the resemblance to the neck of a goose was more than mere coincidence; goose barnacles were thought to be the embryos of barnacle geese, a small species that winters in Europe. Again, people were making what was, for them, an educated guess. No one ever saw a barnacle goose nest (the breeding grounds are in the far arctic), and the bird's black-and-white plumage was thought to match the light and dark plates of the barnacle.

Through a Glass, Darkly

Drawing moralistic lessons from the natural world has a long history, predating Aesop's well-known tales. The alleged vanity of the peacock was held up to condemnation, with the smug reminder not to emulate the bird. Geese represented foolishness, eagles courage and nobility, chickens timidity. There is still the bluebird of happiness, the ostrich with its head in the sand (the real bird never does this), and the stupid turkey. Pelicans, mistakenly believed to feed their starving young on their own blood, were medieval symbols of sacrifice—an emblem adopted by the Christian church in the Dark Ages.

Biblical Birds

The Bible is rich with references to birds, from the stirring poetry of the Old Testament, with its imagery of swift eagles and the like, to the New Testament use of the white dove as the symbol of purity and the Holy Spirit.

Noah released a dove from the ark, and it returned bearing a sprig of olive. (According to legend, the raven shirked the same duty, and was changed from white to black in punishment.) In 1 Kings, God sent ravens to feed the prophet Elijah, who was hiding from King Ahab and Queen Jezebel.

Barn owls, which are common throughout Eurasia and the Middle East, were among the "unclean" birds that the ancient Jews were forbidden to eat.

Not surprisingly, considering the times, predators were disliked, as were scavengers—a bias that is clear in the Bible. Jews were prohibited from eating a wide variety of wild birds, including hawks, owls, crows, gulls, vultures, and eagles; the bat was also included on the list of unclean birds, a taxonomic goof that people still make to this day.

Biblical translations can cause misunderstanding, the most famous of which is the line from the Song of Solomon: ". . . the time of the singing of birds is come, and the voice of the turtle is heard in our land." Turtles are, of course, silent except for a hiss or two; what Solomon was referring to was the turtle *dove,* whose musical coos are a sign of spring over most of Eurasia.

A similar mixup occurs in some translations of the lists of birds that were considered unclean by the Jews. The Hebrew name *bath yannah* was translated as "ostrich," an unlikely choice, but more modern scholars believe it refers to the eagle owl.

◆　◆　◆

♪ 7 ♪

PEOPLE AND BIRDS

Forget the stereotype of the little old lady in tennis shoes sneaking through the woods to watch birdies. Today's bird-watchers—"birders," if you don't mind—are as diverse a lot as you'll find anywhere: yuppies with $1,000 binoculars; school kids with their first field guides in hand; retired couples traveling from refuge to refuge in mobile homes; competitive birders trying to beat other teams by seeing the most birds in a single day; backyard bird feeders who can't tell a chickadee from a finch but enjoy them nonetheless; specialists who love to watch hawks but disdain songbirds, or who like songbirds but are left cold by ducks.

And there are still even a few little old ladies in tennis shoes out there.

For millions of people, birds mean more than pleasant background music on a spring day—they are an integral part of the joy in life, and a bridge between the human and natural world. Their comings and goings unite us with the horizons, just as the rough-legged hawk, sitting in a snowy tree across the field from my house as I write this, unites me with the far arctic tundra. Few other living creatures exert such a hold on the human imagination, or play so great a role in our lives.

◆　◆　◆

For millions of people, birds are more than a pleasant diversion—they are an important bridge between the modern world and natural history. In addition, birders spend billions of dollars annually on gear, books, birdseed, as well as travel; here, birders watch passing hawks along the Kittatinny Ridge in Pennsylvania, a major migration corridor.

A Bonanza in Birding Bucks

In 1985, the last time the Census Bureau took a survey of wildlife-related activities, more than 82 million Americans were lugging home bags of sunflower seed and filling bird feeders. The numbers have undoubtedly risen at the same explosive rate since then, making bird-feeding and bird-watching one of the fastest-growing pastimes. With that growth has come the realiza-tion that birding is big business, too; the Census Bureau estimated that some $14 billion a year is spent on binoculars, bird seed, camera gear, and the like by "non-consumptive" users of wildlife, particularly birders.

Birding can have a tremendous economic impact on communities, as well. Point Pelee in Ontario, a world-famous hotspot for migrating birds, attracts birders who spend nearly $4 million (Canadian) each year in the area on food, lodging, and gear.

Competitive Birding

The traditional view is that bird-watching is a genteel pursuit, with veterans offering generous help to beginners. That image is true, by and large, but not in competitive birding. Then, the gloves come off.

Competitive birding as such is a fairly recent development, although, given human nature, its genesis was probably inevitable. The seeds were always there, in the smugness of a birder who spots a rare bird that everyone else has missed, or has a bigger life list; or in the "can-you-top-this" turn that bird-watching conversations often take. Variations on the theme spring up with each passing season, but most center on who can see the greatest number of species in a set period of time, usually a day. The World Series of Birding, a spinoff from traditional the "Big Day" approach to bird-watching, has become the most hotly contested birding match. Teams of crack birders, sponsored by birding groups, conservation organizations, binocular manufacturers, nature magazines, and others, take to the field in New Jersey each May for a 24-hour blitz, hoping to compile the biggest list and win one of two trophies—including a pair of binoculars embedded in granite. The series motto is "Competition in the name of fun, glory and conservation (but mostly for the fun)." Obviously, the world series doesn't take itself too seriously.

The teams do, though. Routes are mapped out weeks in advance, rare birds located beforehand, timetables drawn up. At the stroke of midnight the birders begin, listening for owls and such night-calling birds as black rails.

Most teams have solicited pledges from noncompetitors, so much per species, with the money going toward conservation, win or lose (about $150,000 in 1989). The Holy Grail of the world series is cracking the 200-species mark—quite a feat, considering there are usually only about 260 varieties of birds in New Jersey at that time of year. In the 1989 contest, the Bausch & Lomb/Chapman Club team won with 201 species, short of the all-time, single-team record of 205 established in 1987. In '89, however, the 31 teams participating spotted a total of 258 species, setting a new record in that respect.

Christmas Bird Counts

The granddaddy of competitive birding is also its mildest incarnation, the annual National Audubon Society Christmas Bird Count, a Yuletide feature since 1900. The idea is simple: Teams try to count as many species and individual birds within a 15-mile circle, sometime between the middle of December and the first week of January. Started as an alternative to the traditional rural Christmas hunt, the CBC (as it is known to aficionados) has grown to include counts from arctic Alaska to Hawaii and Brazil.

A few statistics from the 89th CBC, as reported in the Audubon journal *American Birds:* 42,671 participants, including 6,874 who tallied birds at their feeders, took part in 1,563 counts, racking up a total of more than 66 million birds—down from 193 million the year before. (The drastic decline was blamed on colder weather and shifting roost habits of huge blackbird flocks in the

South, which apparently moved outside the count circles.) The CBC north of Mexico with the highest species total was Santa Barbara, California, with 218; followed by Freeport, Texas, at 208; and Moss Landing, California, with 207. South of the border, the top tropical count was the Atlantic Canal Area in Panama, with 341.

The all-around low count was at Prudhoe Bay, conducted in the twilight of the Alaskan winter with temperatures just above zero. For their efforts, two counters found 15 birds, all ravens.

Life Lists

There are really only two kinds of birders in the world: those that keep lists, and those that don't.

Listers (also know as tickers or, in England, twitchers) are compulsive about tabulating what they've seen. They may keep trip lists, property lists, state and country lists, Big Day lists, CBC lists, feeder lists, monthly, weekly, or seasonal lists. But the most common list of all is the life list.

A life list is nothing more than a record of all the species a birder has seen, usually with a note of the date and location, and even those who abhor the idea of treating birds like inventory generally keep one. A new bird is referred to as a "lifer."

For a North American birder who's done some traveling around the continent, a life list of 350 to 450 is about average. Not everyone is content to be average, however. Some aspire to join the elite "700 Club," those who have seen at least 700 of North America's 800-plus species. Others with the time and money to travel can do even better.

For a while, the king of listers was Norman Chesterfield of Ontario, who has seen 6,364 species of birds worldwide. He was deprived of his crown in 1989, however, when a Swiss birder named Harvey Gilston reached a total of 6,514—out of a world total of about 9,000 species.

Big Crowd, Little Bird

Like avid listers in North America, "twitchers" in Britain will go to great lengths to see a new bird. When a golden-winged warbler—a North American species never before seen in Europe—showed up at a housing development at Maidstone in southeast England, more than 2,000 people descended on the community to see it. Police were forced to use bullhorns to control the crowd, which included birders from as far away as the Netherlands and Belgium.

Feathered Royalty

In the rigidly class-oriented society of pre-European Hawaii, the highest chiefs wore cloaks, helmets, and capes made of fine netting covered with shimmering layers of bird feathers.

The garments are astonishing for their beauty and craftsmanship, but exacted a high price from the birds unlucky enough to bear feathers deemed fit for a king. A single cloak might contain a half-million feathers plucked from up to 90,000 birds. Some birds, like the 'o'o, were trapped, their few yellow side feathers removed, and then released. Others, like the red 'i'iwi, were covered in usable plumage, and so were killed and completely plucked.

Falconry

People have eaten birds since the first *Australopithecus* beaned a flamingo with a rock along the shores of an ancient African lake. Bird bones are hollow and don't fossilize well, but enough have been found in prehistoric human garbage heaps to make it clear that we have been eating fowl for a long, long time.

Much of the pressure was taken off wild birds by the domestication of the chicken (and, to a lesser extent, the pigeon), but mankind kept the hankering for a tasty partridge or duck every now and again. The problem was getting the meal; birds are mobile and fast, and until the advent of firearms, catching them was a tricky business. Nets and snares worked, especially for shorebirds and geese. Songbirds were (and in some areas still are) caught on poles smeared with sticky birdlime. But the most elegant method of all was falconry—using birds to catch birds.

No one knows where or precisely when falconry started, but the best guess places it in China around 2,000 B.C.; the practice also arose, probably independently, in the Mediterranean basin around the same time. It is not surprising that the species that tamed wolves and made them partners in the hunt should do the same with hawks, but there is a crucial difference—through thousands of years of falconry, the hawks, eagles, and falcons were never domesticated. To this day, a "passage" falcon, one captured during its first migration, is considered superior to an "eyas" bird taken from the nest as a chick.

The hawk is trained to fly from the fist or "wait on" high above the ground, while the falconer and a dog flush the game. The hawk is free and untethered, connected to the falconer by the most tenuous bond of hunger, training, and a degree of affection. When the kill is made the falconer allows the hawk to feed, although he may pocket the game and give his partner less prized meat instead.

The Arabs raised falconry to its highest level, but to this day the other "Sport of Kings" is thought of as a medieval European pursuit, introduced by knights of the Crusades who learned it in the Holy Land. There was a complicated set of rules, regulations and etiquette, prescribing what social station could fly what hawk or falcon to what prey. Cruelly, the peasant class, which had the greatest need for protein in their diet, were not allowed to practice this method of procuring wild meat. Perhaps just as well, for royal guardianship protected the birds of prey for centuries; harming them was often punishable by death.

(Box continues on next page)

Peregrine falcons, whose speed and agility are legendary, have been a favorite with falconers since the sport's earliest days in Asia and the Middle East. The peregrine usually makes its kill after a long, fast dive known as a stoop; ducks are a common prey item, as in this famous painting by Audubon.

While no longer the sole purview of the aristocracy, falconry still uses exactly the same techniques that were pioneered thousands of years ago. The sport today is every bit as strictly controlled as it was following the Norman Conquest, although now it is by state and federal wildlife agencies concerned that demand for falconry birds will deplete wild stocks already pressured by human encroachment.

Falcons, especially peregrines and gyrfalcons, are still prized for their searing stoops and lightning-fast kills, and are flown to waterfowl and open-land gamebirds like pheasants. Goshawks and Cooper's hawks, the forest hunters, are often used for rabbits, grouse, and other agile prey. In North America, the hands-down favorite is the red-tailed hawk—common, calm, and able to handle a wide variety of quarry; the same goes for the rarer Harris' hawk of the Southwest.

Despite this extravagant use of feathers, the cloak-makers apparently did little harm to Hawaii's bird populations. The same cannot be said of the Europeans and North Americans who came to the islands, starting in the late 1700s, and cleared the forests, introduced alien predators and competing bird species. Dozens of native Hawaiian birds have since become extinct, including the favorite for feather cloaks, the mamo. The Kauai 'o'o is down to a single individual, but ironically the red 'i'iwi, the species traditionally killed for cloaks, is still fairly common.

Stamps for Ducks

It seems ironic, at first thought, that the North American birds most avidly sought by hunters are the same species that have done rather well in the face of human development. The reason is enlightened self-interest, perhaps best illustrated by duck stamps.

In the waning years of the nineteenth century, unregulated shooting of waterfowl, especially for market, had decimated ducks and geese across the United States and Canada. Using cannon-sized punt guns mounted to the bows of small boats, market hunters could discharge a single blast that would kill or cripple hundreds of swimming ducks, and spring shooting reduced the birds even further. Sport hunters and conservationists (frequently one in the same) managed to halt the worst excesses, but by the 1930s it was apparent that protection alone wasn't going to be enough.

Waterfowl, like these mallards, are among the most heavily managed wild birds in North America, since they are so important to sport hunters. Money from licenses, duck stamps, and taxes have funded land acquisition and research into virtually every facet of their lives.

A painting of a pair of canvasbacks graced the 1990 Pennsylvania waterfowl management stamp, which is sold by the state Game Commission to raise money for wetlands conservation. Ducks frequently serve as the standard-bearers in wetlands conservation, attracting money to save habitat important to other species of plants and animals.

The Dust Bowl drought had dried up the pothole region of the northcentral U.S. and Canadian prairies, where 70 percent of the continent's waterfowl breed. Farmers and ranchers had recklessly drained marshes or fouled the waters. Money was needed to buy up land and restore it for waterfowl. But in the depths of the Depression, there was little money for wildlife.

The answer was the Federal Migratory Bird Hunting and Conservation Stamp, essentially a federal waterfowl hunting license. Introduced in 1934 at a cost of $1, it was required for all duck hunters, with the proceeds going for land acquisition and habitat improvement. The duck stamp's strongest supporters were duck hunters, who realized that without quick action, their sport was doomed.

To call the idea a success is a gross understatement. Over the years, duck stamps (now $12.50 each) have raised tens of millions of dollars, most of which has funded the U.S. National Wildlife Refuge system. Drought and development still threaten waterfowl, but without the money from duck stamps, it is a safe bet that the flocks would be only a memory for old-timers.

The Bard's Birds

People love birds for many reasons, but certainly one of the oddest reasons belonged to the members of the American

Acclimatization Society, an obscure group of New Yorkers in the late 1800s, Obscure, that is, except for one act, an act that modern birders find difficult to forgive.

The American Acclimatization Society was made up of Shakespeare fans, particularly a man named Eugene Scheifflen. Not content to simply enjoy reading the Bard's works, the group's goal was to introduce to the United States every bird mentioned in his writings. Unfortunately, in one line of one play *(Henry IV)*, Shakespeare mentions the European starling—a noisy, aggressive, depressingly adaptable bird. In the Bard's day starlings were apparently common but not pestiferous, a situation that changed with the warmer winters of the nineteenth century. By 1890, when the AAS released a crate of 60 in Central Park, the starling had taken Europe by storm, forming flocks of millions. In retrospect, what followed shouldn't have surprised anyone.

Two earlier releases had failed (as had dozens of introductions by others around the United States), but for the AAS, the third time was the charm. The 60 expatriates settled down and did what starlings do best—rearing more starlings, and raising a messy, noisy ruckus along the way. By the turn of the century they had expanded beyond the city, slowly at first, then with greater and greater momentum—a rolling tide of starlings spreading out like an oil slick from Central Park. They reached the mid-Atlantic states by 1920, covered the eastern United States and Canada by 1925, conquered the Plains by 1940, the Pacific Coast by 1950, and hit southeastern Alaska a few years later. Starlings now occupy most of North America from northern Mexico to the edge of the Arctic. They have visited untold harm on native birds, especially by stealing scarce nest holes; starlings are a major reason for the decline of the eastern bluebird.

The Utilitarian Bird

As the previous chapter made clear, birds have always been important to the spiritual life of primitive people. The same can as easily be said for the day-to-day life as well.

For the Indians of the northern Plains, the golden eagle held a special place of reverence; its mottled tail feathers were used to decorate shields, lances, and scalp locks, as well as the famous headdress that has, erroneously, come to be associated with all Native Americans. The eagle was considered an embodiment of bravery, and its plumage a channel through which men could communicate with spirits. But first, they had to catch them.

A great deal of ritual and preparation went in to catching eagles, and it was grueling, dangerous work. It was considered almost sacrilegious to shoot an eagle with a bow, so pit traps were used instead. An eagle trapper went to a high bluff with good visibility. After digging a hole deep enough to conceal himself, he dragged the soil far off and scattered it to leave no trace. The top of the pit was roofed over with loose sticks and grass, and a large chunk of bloody buffalo meat was tied down to it; often the stuffed skin of a coyote or wolf was erected next to the meat.

The night before trapping, the man would purify himself in the smoke of

The shuffling dance and upright tail feathers of the male sage grouse were the inspiration for some of the dances of the Plains tribes, who drew many of their steps from the movements of wild animals. Dancers would strap a "bustle" of fanned grouse feathers to their waist, capturing some of the flash of the courting bird.

burning sweet grass. Before dawn he would enter the trap, having neither eaten nor drunk. With him he would take a human skull, so its ghost would protect him from injury. As a further precaution, the man's wife would not use her sewing awl during the day, since to do so would invite danger.

Golden eagles are skilled hunters, but they scavenge freely, and the sight of a wolf feeding on a chunk of meat would soon attract one. When the eagle finally landed on the roof of the pit, the hunter would carefully reach up through the sticks and grab its powerful feet, then pull the eagle into the blind. Flailing with its seven-foot wings and trying desperately to grab with its talons, the eagle would be a very real danger until the hunter could break its neck. A skilled eagle trapper would sometimes catch ten in a day. (Precisely the same technique of pit-trapping was used more than a century later by biologists trying to catch the last wild Calfornia condors for radio-tagging; there's no word on whether they carried human skulls for protection.)

The bowing, shuffling dance of courting sage grouse and sharp-tailed grouse in the American West provided the inspiration for several Plains Indian dances, as well as the "bustle," a fan of long feathers belted behind at the waist. The bustle mimics the raised, pointed tail feathers of the cock grouse, although the associations are so old that many of the original meanings have been lost.

Feathers have figured prominently in human dress, up to and including the ostrich-feather boa. The varied plumes of the birds of paradise are prized by highlanders in Papua New Guinea, and the cloaks of the Hawaiians and the headdresses of the Crow Indians have been mentioned, but feather dress may have reached its zenith among the ancient Maya of Central America.

Unfortunately, the Classic Maya civilization had all but collapsed even before the Spanish conquered the Yucatán Peninsula. But we have the Mayan's carvings and wall paintings, which show a flamboyant use of feathers in capes and cloaks, fans, and parasols, but especially in headdresses overflowing with the long green tail plumes of the resplendent quetzal, the red or yellow feathers of macaws. Ceremonial battle gear shimmered with the plumage of jungle birds; for this description we can thank the Spanish armies, who noted the beauty of their enemy's dress even as they crushed the Mayan resistance and subjugated their culture.

From Jungle to Freezer

What would holidays be without birds, at least on the table? Americans consume millions of turkeys each Thanksgiving, and untold chickens and turkeys throughout the year, but these dietary stalwarts arrived in the kitchen from strikingly different routes.

The chicken was first domesticated in India more than 5,000 years ago— not in its current white, chunky incarnation, but as the wild red jungle fowl, a lanky bird with red-orange hackles and long, curving green tail plumes. The jungle fowl is a member of the pheasant family, still a resident of tropical forests from India to Indochina. Why it was domesticated, and not one of the dozens of other pheasant species native to the same region, is a mystery, but the results prove it to have been the right choice. Domestic chickens spread—from trader to seafarer to barnyard—northwest to the Mediterranean, up to Europe, into the Middle East and Asia. When the Polynesians set out in their great outrigger sea canoes, they carried chickens along with their taro shoots and pigs.

Chickens did not reach the New World, but the sedentary cultures of the Southwest and Central America had a domestic fowl of their own, the turkey—common turkeys in the United States and northern Mexico, the ocellated turkey in the Maya region of the Yucatán. Spaniards carried domesticated common turkeys from Mexico to Europe, where they were an instant hit in every royal court and humble farm. It is an irony of history that European colonists arriving in North America a century later brought with them domestic turkeys reared back home—much easier to convert into supper than a woods-wise wild gobbler.

Cormorant Co-workers

Fish are good to eat but hard to catch. Cormorants excel at catching fish, but aren't usually inclined to share their

Words from Birds

Birds have added a lot to the language, especially in expressions:

Like water off a duck's back. Waterfowl have a large gland at the base of the tail that supplies the oil they preen into their feathers, giving them water repellency. A petroleum oil spill, however, can so foul their feathers that they lose their insulation and buoyancy.

Birds of a feather flock together. At least most of the time. In the winter, mixed songbird flocks are common, but even on refuges where hundreds of thousands of ducks and geese gather, each species stays pretty much with its own kind.

Eagle-eyed is valid, *wise as an owl* isn't, and anyone who *eats like a bird* is going to be obese in very short order, since birds consume up to 20 percent of their body weight daily. *Happy as a lark* refers to that bird's exuberant song-flight, but even larks have bad days, when troubles come home to roost, giving them *something to grouse about,* so to speak. Loons aren't mad, but their yodeling call sounds that way—hence *crazy as a loon.* And *swan song* comes from the belief that the mute swan, silent all its life, sings a song just as it is about to die.

Birds of a feather don't *always* flock together; in this case, laughing gulls, herring gulls, red knots, and ruddy turnstones mix while feeding on horseshoe crab eggs along the Delaware Bay.

meal with humans. The answer? Trained cormorants are collared so that they can catch fish, but can't swallow them completely.

Once a common practice in much of the Orient, cormorant-fishing has all but died out, except in China. Here, tenders still tie leashes to the loose-fitting collars on their birds and send them into the murky water. When the cormorant catches a fish it swallows it, but the fish cannot go farther than the throat. As a dozen or more cormorants dive and surface around his boat, the tender in turn pulls each one in, makes it cough up the fish in its throat, then returns it to the water. In some areas the fishing is done at night, in the harsh light of burning wood and pitch in a metal basket that protrudes over the bow of the boat.

What a cormorant produces at the end opposite the mouth is of paramount concern in South America, where for more than 150 years the dried guano of the guanay cormorant has been collected from the ground around the bird's breeding colonies and converted into fertilizer. A similar industry occurred in coastal Africa.

Peru learned a hard lesson in ecology and economics from the guanay. The guano industry, one of the country's important cash sources, was dependent on the 15 million cormorants nesting along the edge of the cold Pacific, where they fed on unbelievably abundant anchovies. Periodically, though, the unpredictable shift of ocean currents called "El Niño" would force the anchovies from inshore waters, and the cormorant population would plummet until the fish returned and good breeding conditions were restored.

In the 1960s Peru began fishing for anchovies, taking up to 15 million tons a year. The anchovies, seriously overfished, declined in number, taking the guanay with them. Fishermen, unwilling to see their own hand in the mess, blamed the remaining birds and called for their extermination. Cooler heads eventually prevailed, but human greed decimated not one, but two important industries, and seriously damaged the marine food chain in the bargain.

Saved by the Birds

The Mormon colonists in Utah were having a bad spring in 1848—first floods, then late frosts. Now, their crops—and their chances of survival—were disappearing under waves of long-horned grasshoppers, better known as crickets.

Help came from the skies, in one of the most famous incidents of birds aiding people. Thousands of California gulls—"more of them until the heavens darkened with them," in the words of a witness—descended on the grasshopper hordes and starting eating. The crops were saved that year, and again in the same fashion in 1855.

The Mormons credited the gulls' appearance to divine intercession, while biologists are more inclined to speak of the lure that abundant food resources have for wandering predators like the gulls. Regardless, the grateful Mormons erected a monument topped with two golden gulls in Salt Lake City.

Columbus also got an assist from birds, at a crucial moment on his first voyage. With his crew about to mutiny, Columbus sighted a flock of landbirds passing overhead, which he correctly argued meant that land was near at hand. At the time he was more than 700 miles from land, and the birds were undoubtedly songbirds making the giant, over-water leap from the Northeast coast to South America.

In Memorium

Most bird names are straightforward and descriptive; there is no ambiguity about the appearance of a red-winged blackbird, for instance. But Brewer's blackbird begs the question—just who was Brewer, anyway?

He was Thomas Mayo Brewer, a Boston physician and a friend of Audubon's, who is immortalized by two North American birds; Brewer's blackbird and Brewer's sparrow, both western species. His friend Audubon tried a third time, naming what he thought was a new kind of duck after him. Unfortunately, the "bemaculated duck," as Audubon also called it, was merely a hybrid between a mallard and a gadwall.

There are 77 North American birds named for people, from Abert's towhee to Xantus' murrelet. Most are western or northern, for a good reason—birds of the eastern colonies were known by colloquial names generations before serious naturalists began studying them. But as explorers penetrated the wilderness in the 1800s, the scientists accompanying them had an opportunity to name their newest finds in honor of friends, colleagues, collectors, and financial supporters.

Baird's sandpiper memorializes Spencer Fullerton Baird, secretary of the Smithsonian in the 1880s; Swainson's

Spencer Fullerton Baird, secretary of the Smithsonian in the 1880s and a respected naturalist, is memorialized by the Baird's sandpiper, an arctic species.

hawk, thrush, and warbler are named for William Swainson, an erratic British naturalist; and Xantus' murrelet commemorates John Xantus, a Hungarian ornithologist with a fair dose of con man in his makeup (he once claimed to have been a U.S. naval captain, basing that contention on a stint as a tide observer along the Pacific coast).

With four birds named for him (a storm-petrel, plover, phalarope, and warbler), Alexander Wilson is better enshrined in field guides than any other person. Although not as well known today as Audubon, Wilson had an arguably greater impact on early American ornithology, and his illustrated *American Ornithology* preceded Audubon's work by many years.

No other group of birds has as many members named for people as the sparrows—9 out of 33 species. Perhaps the reason has to do with the overall drabness of sparrow plumage; naming a new bird for a friend is an alternative to calling it "yet another brown, striped sparrow."

Some honorees have, alas, lost their place in the sun. A few years back, the American Ornithologists' Union decided that the myrtle warbler of the East and the Audubon's warbler of the West were races of the same species, which they lumped under the name of yellow-rumped warbler, leaving John James with only the Audubon's shearwater to carry his name. The Rivoli's hummingbird has since been rechristened the magnificent hummingbird, and Weid's crested flycatcher is more prosaically known today as the brown-crested flycatcher. Sometimes the opposite holds true. In 1858, two color forms of the western grebe were described as separate species, the western and the Clark's grebe. They were lumped together for years, but in the late 1980s were split again into two species because they do not interbreed.

♦ ♦ ♦

ODDS AND ENDS

Bizarre courtship, weird nests, odd food habits, ancient legends—what's left to say about birds? Plenty, of course, because birds are relentlessly surprising. In Tibet, snow finches nest in the burrows of pikas (a relative of the rabbit, smaller in size), returning year after year to the same colonies. A species of New Guinean parrot eats nothing but fungi. The salivary glands of yellow-shafted flickers are unusually big, producing lots of saliva to neutralize the formic acid excreted by ants, the flicker's main food. Birds are astonishing animals in just about every respect.

◆ ◆ ◆

Hoat'z a Hoatzin?

One of the most striking features of the fossils of *Archaeopteryx,* the first bird, is the presence of reptilian and avian anatomy in one creature. But you needn't look only in rocks millions of years old for this juxtaposition. Instead, look at the hoatzin.

The hoatzin (the name is Aztec and is pronounced "hoe-at-sin") is a very peculiar bird, so peculiar that it has been hailed as a living fossil. As near as any-one can tell, this slim, brown jungle bird with a shaggy crest fits in somewhere between the pheasants and the cranes on the avian tree of life, but its exact relationship to the rest of the bird world has been contested for a long time. A resident of the Amazon basin, the hoatzin is one of the only birds known that eats nothing but leaves, which it grinds up not in its gizzard like most birds, but in its out-sized crop, which takes up nearly a third of the bird's chest area.

Why is leaf-eating so rare? Because leaves contain a maximum of tough cellulose and a minimum of nutrition, so any animal that eats them must eat a great deal in order to stay alive, and must develop a way to digest them. The hoatzin has borrowed a trick from cows—it ferments the leaves in its crop with the help of symbiotic bacteria. But the hoatzin's diet isn't the most unusual aspect of its biology, nor is its habit of nesting in large colonies along river, or its chick's ability to swim. The oddest thing about the hoatzin is its claws.

The young chick, cloaked in reddish down and already sporting a Mohawk-style crest of dark feathers, has two claws at the joint of each wing—at what was, in its reptilian ancestors, the end of the foreleg. The claws are temporary, and disappear after a few weeks, but they serve the chick well while they last (it is interesting to note that many birds have claws as embryos, but lose them before hatching). Poor fliers even as adults, hoatzin chicks are expert climbers, scrambling through the mangroves at the least disturbance. It isn't hard to see how an *Archaeopteryx* could have gotten around in the same manner.

KIKI-DOO TO YOU, TOO

The easiest way to remember a bird song is to syllabify it, changing the tune into words. The result are sometimes nonsensical, sometimes hilarious, but always imaginative.

American bittern: *Oonga-chunk, oonga-chunk!*

Black rail: *Kiki-doo, kiki-doo, kiki-doo.*

Willet: *Pee-wee willET, pee-wee willET.*

Willow ptarmigan: *Tobacco, tobacco.*

Barred owl: *Who cooks for you, who cooks for you all-l-l-l?*

Olive-sided flycatcher: *Hic! three beers.*

Tufted titmouse: *Peter, peter, peter, peter.*

Warbling vireo: *When I sees one I shall seize one and I'll squeeze it 'till it SQUIRTS!*

Chestnut-sided warbler: *Pleased, pleased, pleased to meet'cha* or *See, see, see, see Miss Beecher.*

Yellow warbler: *Sweet sweet sweet I'm so sweet.*

Common yellowthroat: *Witchity, witchity, witchity which.*

Ovenbird: *tea-cher tea-CHER TEA-CHER TEA-CHER!*

Eastern meadowlark: *Spring of the year!*

Cardinal: *To-whit, to-whit, to-whit, what-cheer, what-cheer, what-cheer.*

American goldfinch: *Potato-chip, potato-chip.*

Rufous-sided towhee: *Drink your tea-a-a-a!*

White-throated sparrow: *Oh sweet Canada, Canada, Canada.*

Razorbill: *Hey Al!*

The easiest way to remember bird songs is to convert the syllables to words; thus, the song of the eastern meadowlark becomes "Spring of the Ye-e-e-e-ar!"

Early Bird Artists

The earliest representations of birds by humans are on rock art left by Paleolithic hunters in Europe, Africa, and Australia. Some are stylized, some dramatically lifelike, and all were probably ritualistic in nature, invoking the spirits of the animals to aid in the hunt.

Birds have been a common motif ever since. Ancient Egyptian tomb paintings show men casting nets for waterfowl and capturing herons with throwing sticks. As already mentioned, the Egyptians worshiped a pantheon of bird-related gods like Horus, which appear in their paintings and sculpture. But even through the Middle Ages and Renaissance, birds were usually consigned to the fringes of art—decorative features flitting about landscapes, rather than subjects worthy of serious attention.

That attitude began to change at the same time that exploration was opening up the New World, as well as the remote corners of Africa and Asia. In North America, explorer/artists like Mark Catesby and Alexander Wilson were bringing to light novelties of plant and animal life, especially birds. But Catesby and Wilson painted in the style of their day, depicting the birds rigidly, usually in stiff profile, without the spark of life.

Then came Audubon.

Vain, conceited, and more than a bit of a liar, John James Audubon was born in Santo Domingo, the illegitimate son of a French naval officer. In 1803, at the age of eighteen, he was shipped off to America by his father, in the hope that he would make something of himself. He failed in retailing and left his family for long stretches of time while he explored his adopted land, but in the process, he married bird art and ornithology, infusing both with a life and exuberance they had long been missing.

Audubon's style was revolutionary for its time; he painted birds as they appeared in nature—moving, living, breathing birds that threatened to fly off the very page. His compositions were dramatic, his settings accurate (although many of the botanical backgrounds were painted by skilled assistants like Joseph Mason). In one, a golden eagle soars above jagged mountains, clutching a snowshoe hare in its talons. In another, two peregrine falcons feed voraciously on their prey. Yellow-breasted chats fill the air in courtship flight. Wood chips fly as ivory-billed woodpeckers hunt for beetle larvae. A whip-poor-will chases a multicolored cecropia moth through the leaves of an oak tree. Here is reality, Audubon's paintings say to the viewer.

(Box continues on next page)

Audubon observed the white phase of the gyrfalcon in Labrador in 1833, but did not paint them until much later, working (as he usually did) from specimens.

Nº 17. Plate 82.

Drawn from Nature & Published

John J. Audubon F.R.S. F.L.S. &c

Caprimulgus vociferus

Whip-poor-will.   Male 1. Female 2.

quercus tinctoria

Ridge Black Oak.

Accuracy and vibrant composition were Audubon's hallmarks, shown here in his painting of whip-poor-wills. His style was a rebellion against the artistic conventions of the day, which called for stiff, formalized poses in natural history illustrations.

John James Audubon was vain and arrogant, but he revolutionized bird art by placing his subjects in their natural habitat—a tradition that continues today.

His self-imposed task was to paint every species of North American bird, and he pushed himself mercilessly, traveling from Labrador to the Dry Tortugas and west up the Missouri River into Indian country. He did not paint every species, of course, but he painted hundreds, many that he discovered himself. The publication of his double-folio of paintings, *The Birds of America,* was justly hailed as a masterpiece.

Audubon's work (with Wilson's) greatly influenced a young artist of the next generation. Louis Agassiz Fuertes, born near Albany, New York, almost a century after Audubon, had a twin fascination for art and wildlife from the earliest age. While studying at Cornell, his work caught the eye of Elliot Coues, one of the most influential ornithologists of the early twentieth century, who boldly told the American Ornithologists' Union that the mantle of Audubon had fallen on Fuertes' shoulders.

Audubon may today be the better known of the two, but artistically and scientifically, Fuertes's work far surpasses Audubon's. His watercolors have an absolute authenticity, the result of a finely honed technique and an eye that translated form and motion into two dimensions without losing the vibrancy of the live bird. Where Audubon pursued his private vision, Fuertes was the consummate illustrator, turning out thousands of paintings for magazines and books, including *Birds of New York* and *Birds of Massachusetts and Other New England States.*

Toward the end of his life, Fuertes began doing more and more larger, almost impressionistic oils, confiding to friends that this was his favorite style. Tragically, he was not to continue; Fuertes was killed in a railway crossing accident in 1927, at age 53. To many, he remains the most accomplished bird artist that North America has ever produced.

Unkind Ravens, and Other Avian Aggregations

A bunch of birds is called a flock, right? Not always. Depending on the species, you may have:

A parliament of owls
An ostentation of peacocks
An unkindness of ravens
A covey of quail
A gaggle of geese
A fall of woodcock
A pitying of turtle doves
A cast of hawks
A murmuration of starlings
A congress of crows
A flight of swallows
An exultation of larks

Cleanliness Is Next to Godliness

Birds' nests are usually unsanitary places, even when the chick can defecate over the edge, as most hawks and eagles do, or void a fecal sac that the adults can carry off, as is the case with many songbirds. But the situation is much worse if the nest is down inside a tree cavity, and if the chicks are as messy as owlets.

It's not just droppings. There are pieces of uneaten meals, old regurgitated pellets, even the mummified remains of dead chicks. And many nest holes are used year after year, so the debris builds up in a mat at the bottom on the hole. Conditions like that are an invitation to insects, especially bluebottle flies, which lay their eggs in the filth. The larvae feed on the blood of the chicks, sometimes infesting nests so heavily that the babies are killed.

Screech-owls in Texas have devised a unique way of beating the problem, though. They catch blind snakes—small, wormlike burrowers—and carry them back to their nest holes alive. Released in the nest, the snakes burrow down through the accumulated junk and eat the bluebottle fly grubs. Researchers have found that owlets from snake-patrolled nests grow bigger and faster, and die less frequently then those from holes without such unusual protection.

Building Birdboxes

Building and erecting birdboxes is a fun, easy way to help the bird life in your neighborhood, but to be successful, the box must be tailored to the species you want to attract. Each bird has its own requirements for habitat, box size, and entrance-hole diameter. For best results, follow the dimensions given in the chart opposite.

Construct nest boxes from untreated 1-inch-thick lumber (2-inch for larger boxes); avoid preserved wood, which may release toxic chemicals when wet, and metal, which acts like an oven in summer. Drill four or five $\frac{1}{4}$-inch drainage holes in the floor, and two similar holes near the top of the sides for ventilation. Never add a perch; nesting birds don't need it and it provides a perching spot for harassing starlings. Build the box with a hinged roof or side so it can be cleaned at the end of each season. Nest boxes do not need to be painted, although an oil stain will help preserve the wood.

Boxes can be used for different species. The bluebird and wren patterns are good for chickadees and titmice, a kestrel box placed in the woods is good for screech and saw-whet owls, and wood duck boxes serve for mergansers. A modified wood duck box, with a 13-inch-wide front and 7-inch-square entrance hole, can be used for shelter by barred owls.

New Bird on the Block

It's always big news in the birding community when a new species of bird is blown off course and winds up in North America. Known as accidentals, such birds send serious bird-listers into fits of ecstasy. But imagine their euphoria when the accidental is a bird that has only been seen in China and Australia—and was only discovered six years before.

That bird was Cox's sandpiper, a close look-alike of the common pectoral sandpiper. It was captured in September 1987, at Duxbury Beach, Massachusetts, by bird-banders with the Manomet Bird Observatory, and in fact was identified at the time as a pectoral, then banded and released. Only later did birders notice that it was different. Not only was it the first recorded sighting in the Northern Hemisphere, but it was the first time the species had been seen in juvenile plumage, suggesting that it had come from the breeding grounds, probably in Siberia.

NEST BOXES

Species	Overall dimensions*	Entrance hole	Placement
Bluebirds (Eastern, western, and mountain)	$9 \times 5\frac{1}{2} \times 5\frac{1}{2}$	$1\frac{1}{2}$	6' high on post in open ground
House wren	$8 \times 5\frac{1}{2} \times 4$	$1\frac{1}{4}$	Head-high in yard or garden
Flicker	$24 \times 7 \times 4\frac{1}{2}$	$2\frac{1}{2}$	Fill box to roof with sawdust; hang in fencerow or orchard
Kestrel	$16 \times 9\frac{1}{2} \times 8$	3	Sawdust on bottom; hang in fencerows, isolated trees
Wood duck	$24 \times 11\frac{1}{2} \times 10$	3×4 oval	Trees along waterways

*Overall dimensions are height, width, depth; all measurements in inches.

Cage Birds

As annoying as they may be, most fads are harmless; after all, a Hula Hoop or pet rock is a pretty innocuous thing. But the current rage for exotic pet birds, especially parrots, has had catastrophic effects on wild bird populations.

Through the 1980s, as many as 800,000 birds were legally imported into the United States each year, and as many as another 100,000 smuggled in. Even that figure is misleading, since many of the erstwhile "legal" birds have murky origins; at one point, Bolivia was exporting—on an annual basis—three times its total population of hyacinth macaws. The birds were really coming from Brazil, where they are protected—smuggled into Bolivia and exported under doctored papers.

The number of birds reaching the United States tells only part of the story. By some estimates, as many as 100 birds die in capture, transit, or quarantine for each one that reaches a U.S. pet store alive. In the jungle, capture techniques are often crude. Chopping down nest trees is a preferred method of getting chicks, a practice that kills adults and infants alike, as well as eliminating scarce nest sites.

Largely because of the pet trade, as many as a third of the parrot and macaw species in Mexico and Central and South America are endangered. One, the Spix's (or little blue) macaw of Brazil, was down to 200 birds in 1986, when scarcity drove the price for a pair to more than $50,000. With that kind of demand, the macaw's fate was sealed, and today it is presumed extinct in the wild, with only about 40 individuals in captivity—most owned by scattered bird collectors, instead of concentrated in a single breeding location.

(Box continues on next page)

Yew Are What Yew Eat

Cedar waxwings have lovely yellow tail tips, or at least most of them do. About 30 years ago, birders started noticing a few waxwings with orange tips, a color form that had never been recorded before. Since then, the numbers of this so-called "burnt-orange" form have increased dramatically.

No one is yet completely sure why this plumage twist should have appeared so suddenly, but some biologists now believe it is a question of diet. The yellow pigment in a normal waxwing tail tip is a canary-xanthophyll, which is metabolized from the bird's diet. But the burnt-orange birds have an additional pigment in the tail, carotenoid rhodoxanthin, which is taken directly from food substances and deposited in growing feathers—perhaps a reason

The problem is not confined to the New World. The cockatoos of Australia and New Guinea have been pet trade targets for years, and one, the all-black palm cockatoo, is critically endangered. Worldwide, collection for the cage bird trade probably surpasses tropical deforestation as the leading danger to parrots and their relatives.

Sadly, captivity is difficult for parrots and macaws, which are intelligent, highly social creatures that need interaction with others of their species. Confined alone in a small cage, many develop neuroses that may result in feather-pulling, screaming, biting, and furniture destruction—hardly the recipe for a happy pet/owner relationship. Small wonder that zoos are flooded with requests to take unwanted pet parrots—requests that can rarely be met, since zoos have limited space and resources.

A few parrots and a larger number of finches breed easily in captivity, and purchasing them does not put pressure on wild populations. New York, which was the first state to prohibit sales of wild-caught birds, recommends the following captive-bred species, especially for first-time bird owners.

Canaries (all varieties)	Cockatiel (all colors)
Zebra finch	Blue-masked lovebird
Lady Gouldian finch	Crimson rosella
Society (Bengalese) finch	Eastern rosella
Java sparrow	Pale-headed (blue) rosella
Diamond dove	Red rumped parrot (all color phases)
Common parakeet (budgerigar)	Bourke's parrot

why most orange-tipped waxwings are young birds. The biologists theorize that in the past three decades waxwings have begun feeding on a new food plant that contains this pigment—a likely candidate is the ornamental yew.

How Long Do Birds Live?

People have always wondered how long wild birds live, but because a chick isn't issued a birth certificate when it hatches, the answer has been hard to come by. A captive European eagle owl lived to age 68, and there are many unproven claims of parrots that lived for a century or more, but such life spans are unlikely for wild birds.

Bird banding is slowly providing answers, though. Millions of birds are ringed each year in the United States and Canada by licensed banders, using

The longevity record for a great blue heron is 23 years, three months, based on the recovery of a Canadian heron banded in 1947. Longevity records can be misleading, however, because most birds live considerably shorter lives than the record-holders.

sequentially numbered aluminum bands. When a bird is recaptured or found dead, the band provides a method of identifying it, and tracking its movement and life span.

Given opposite are longevity records for a number of North American birds, but remember that these are *records;* most birds of any given species live much shorter lives than indicated here, and the average life span of a songbird is less than a year. The banding records

128

RECORDED BIRD LIFESPANS

Species	Age (years, months)	Where banded	When banded
Common loon	7, 10	Ontario	1935
Leach's storm-petrel	29, 00	New Brunswick	1956
Great blue heron	23, 03	Ontario	1947
Canada goose	23, 06	Illinois	1944
Mallard	23, 05	Oregon	1948
Least sandpiper	16, 00	Nova Scotia	1970
Red-tailed hawk	19, 09	Wisconsin	1958
Bald eagle	21, 11	Alaska	1965
Bobwhite	6, 05	Missouri	1954
Herring gull	27, 03	New Brunswick	1949
Mourning dove	19, 04	Colorado	1958
Great horned owl	17, 04	Illinois	1959
Short-eared owl	4, 04	British Columbia	1966
Ruby-throated hummingbird	6,03	Missouri	1970
Downy woodpecker	11, 05	New York	1942
Tree swallow	11, 00	Ontario	1970
Blue jay	18, 04	New York	1963
Scarlet tanager	10, 01	West Virginia	1970
Northern cardinal	15, 09	Pennsylvania	1956
Chipping sparrow	9, 09	Georgia	1929
Swamp sparrow	4, 10	Minnesota	1925
Red-winged blackbird	15, 09	New Jersey	1967

can be misleading; the fact that the oldest blue jay lived a year longer than the oldest great horned owl does not mean that jays, on the whole, live longer than owls—the opposite is more likely true. That jay, like all the other birds on this list, was just plain lucky.

The Final Bird Word

Socrates, going numb from the deadly effects of a bowl of hemlock, saved his last words for a bird, in a manner of speaking: "I owe a cock to Aesculapius. Do not forget to pay it."

◆　◆　◆

PHOTO CREDITS

SELECTED BIBLIOGRAPHY

Andrle, R. F., and J. R. Carroll, eds. 1988. *The Atlas of Breeding Birds of New York State.* Cornell University Press.

Armstrong, Edward A. 1965. *The Ethology of Bird Display and Bird Behavior.* rev. ed. Dover Publications Inc.

Armstrong, Robert H. 1980. *A Guide to Birds of Alaska.* Alaska Northwest Publishing Co.

Attenborough, David. 1987. *The First Eden.* Little, Brown & Co.

Austin, Oliver L. Jr., and Arthur Singer. 1961. *Birds of the World.* Golden Press.

Baker, Robin. 1980 *The Mystery of Migration.* The Viking Press.

Bakker, Robert T. 1986. *The Dinosaur Heresies.* William Morrow and Co., Inc.

Bednarz, James C. 1987. Pair and Group Reproductive Success, Polyandry, and Cooperative Breeding in Harris' Hawks. *The Auk* 104:393–404.

Bednarz, James C. 1987. Successive Nesting and Autumnal Breeding in Harris' Hawks. *The Auk* 104:85–96.

Bednarz, James C. 1988. Cooperative Hunting in Harris' Hawks *(Parabuteo uncinctus).* *Science* 239:1525–1527.

Bednarz, James C. 1988. A Comparative Study of the Breeding Ecology of Harris' and Swainson's Hawks in Southeastern New Mexico. *The Condor* 90:311–323.

Beebe, Frank L. 1984. *A Falconry Manual.* Hancock House Publishers Ltd.

Bent, Arthur Cleveland. 1919–1968, *Life Histories of North American Birds.* reprinted eds. Dover Publications Inc.

Berger, Andrew J. 1971. *Bird Study.* Dover Publications Inc.

Boates, J. S., and R. McNeil. 1984. Longevity Record for the Sanderling. *Journal of Field Ornithology* 55:485.

Brown, Leslie, and Dean Amadon. 1968. *Eagles, Hawks and Falcons of the World.* 2 vols. McGraw-Hill.

Broun, Maurice. 1984. *Hawks Aloft.* Kutztown Publishing Co.

Burton, J. A., ed. 1984. *Owls of the World: Their Evolution, Structure and Ecology.* Tanager Books.

Cade, Thomas J. 1982. *The Falcons of the World.* Cornell University Press.

Clapp, R. B., M. K. Klimkiewicz, and J. H. Kennard. 1982. Longevity Records of North American Birds: Gaviidae through Alcidae. *Journal of Field Ornithology* 53:81–124.

Clapp, R. B., M. K. Klimkiewicz, and A. G. Futcher. 1983. Longevity Records of North American Birds: Columbidae through Paridae. *Journal of Field Ornithology* 54:123–137.

Craighead, J. J., and F. C. Craighead Jr. 1969. *Hawks, Owls and Wildlife.* Dover Publications Inc.

Diamond, A. W., and T. E. Lovejoy, eds. 1985. Conservation of Tropical Forest Birds. *International Council for Bird Preservation Technical Publication* No. 4.

Dorst, Jean. 1974. *The Life of Birds.* Columbia University Press.

Durant, Mary, and Michael Harwood. 1980. *On the Road With John James Audubon.* Dodd, Mead & Co.

Erlich, Paul R., David S. Dobkin, and Darryl Wheye. 1988. *The Birder's Handbook.* Fireside Books.

Feduccia, Alan. 1980. *The Age of Birds.* Harvard University Press.

Fisher, J., and R. T. Peterson. 1969. *The World of Birds.* 2d ed. Crescent Books.

Forsyth, Adrian, and Ken Miyata. 1984. *Tropical Nature.* Charles Scribner's Sons.

Gehlbach, F. R., and R. Baldridge. 1987. Live Blind Snakes *(Leptotyphlops dulcis)* in Eastern Screech Owls *(Otus asio)* Nests: A Novel Commensalism. *Oecologia* 71:560–563.

Godfrey, W. Earl. 1986. *The Birds of Canada.* National Museum of Natural Sciences.

Greenway, J. C. Jr. 1967. *Extinct and Vanishing Birds of the World.* 2d ed. Dover Publications Inc.

Grinnel, George Bird. 1962. *Blackfoot Lodge Tales.* University of Nebraska Press.

Hamerstrom, Frances. 1986. *Harrier, Hawk of the Marshes.* Smithsonian Institution Press.

Harris, Larry D. 1984. *The Fragmented Forest.* University of Chicago Press.

Harrison, Hal H. 1984. *Wood Warbler's World.* Simon & Schuster.

Heckwelder, John. 1971. *History, Manners and Customs of Indian Nations Who Once Inhabited Pennsylvania and the Neighboring States.* reprint ed. Arno Press Inc. and the New York Times.

Hudon, Jocelyn, and A. H. Brush. 1989. Probable Dietary Basis of a Color Variant of the Cedar Waxwing. *Journal of Field Ornithology* 60:361–368.

Jackson, Jerome A. 1986. Biopolitics, Management of Federal Lands and the Conservation of the Red-cockaded Woodpecker. *American Birds* 40:1162–1168.

Johnsgard, Paul A. 1988. *North American Owls.* Smithsonian Institution Press.

Kasprzyk, M. J, R. A. Forster, and B. A. Harrington. 1987. First Northern Hemisphere Record and First Juvenile Plumage Description of the Cox's Sandpiper *(Calidris paramelanotos). American Birds* 41:1359–1364.

Kerlinger, Paul. 1989. *Flight Strategies of Migrating Hawks.* University of Chicago Press.

King, Warren. compiler. 1981. *Endangered Birds of the World: The ICBP Red Data Book.* Smithsonian Institution Press.

Klimkiewicz, M. K., and A. G. Futcher. 1987. Longevity Records of North American Birds: Coebebinae through Estrildidae. Journal of Field Ornithology 558:318–333.

Klimkiewicz, M. K., and A. G. Futcher. 1989. Longevity Records of North American Birds, Supplement 1. *Journal of Field Ornithology* 60:469–494.

Kricher, John C. 1989. *The Neotropical Companion.* Princeton University Press.

Leahy, Christopher. 1984. *The Birdwatcher's Companion.* Bonanza Books.

LeBaron, Geoffrey S. 1989. The 89th Christmas Bird Count. *American Birds* 43:551–559.

Leopold, A. S., R. J. Gutiérrez, and M. T. Bronson. 1981. *North American Game Birds and Animals.* Charles Scribner's Sons.

Marwick, Ernest W. 1975. *The Folklore of Orkney and Shetland.* Rowman and Littlefield.

Miller, E. H., and R. McNeil. 1988. Longevity Records for the Least Sandpiper: A Revision. *Journal of Field Ornithology* 59:403–404.

Morton, E. S., and R. Greenberg. 1989. The Outlook for Migratory Birds: "Future Shock" for Birders. *American Birds* 43:178–183.

Nelson, Bryan. 1979. *Seabirds: Their Biology and Ecology.* A&W Publishers, Inc.

Newton, Ian. 1979. *Population Ecology in Raptors.* Buteo Books.

Owen, Oliver S. 1975. *Natural Resource Conservation.* 2d ed. Macmillan Publishing Co., Inc.

Peck, Robert McCracken. 1982. *A Celebration of Birds: The Life and Art of Louis Agassiz Fuertes.* Walker and Co.

Peterson, Roger Tory. 1979. *Penguins.* Houghton Mifflin Co.

Shortt, Terence M. 1977. *Wild Birds of the Americas.* Houghton Mifflin Co.

Sklepkovych, B. O., and W. A. Montevecchi. 1989. The World's Largest Known Nesting Colony of Leach's Storm-petrels on Baccalieu Island, Newfoundland. *American Birds* 43:38–42.

Tate, James Jr. 1986. The Blue List for 1986. *American Birds* 40:227–236.

Terres, John K. 1980. *The Audubon Society Encyclopeadia of North American Birds.* Alfred A. Knopf.

U.S. Department of the Interior. 1986. *The Breeding Bird Survey: Its First 15 Years, 1965–1979. By Bystrack, Geissler, and Robbins.* U.S. Government Printing Office.

U.S. Fish & Wildlife Service. *1983. Nearctic Avian Migrants in the Neotropics.* U.S. Department of the Interior. By Rappole et al. U.S. Government Printing Office.

Vickery, P. D., D. W. Finch, and P. K. Donahue. 1987. Juvenile Cox's Sandpiper *(Calidris paramelanotos)* in Massachusetts, a First New World Occurence and a Hitherto Undescribed Plumage. *American Birds* 41:1366–1369.

Walker, L. W. 1974. *The Book of Owls.* Alfred A. Knopf.

Wallace, G. J. 1963. *An Introduction to Ornithology.* 2d ed. Macmillan Co.

Walter, Hartmut. 1979. *Eleonara's Falcon: Adaptations to Prey and Habitat in a Social Raptor.* University of Chicago Press.

Welty, Joel C. 1975. *The Life of Birds.* W. B. Saunders Co.

Wilford, John Noble. 1986. *The Riddle of the Dinosaurs.* Alfred A. Knopf.

Wilson, E. O, ed. 1986. *Biodiversity,* National Academy Press.

Wink, J., S. E. Senner, and L. J. Goodrich. 1987. Food Habits of Great Horned Owls. *Proceedings of the Pennsylvania Academy of Science* 61:133–137.

INDEX

Numbers in italics indicate illustrations.